EVERYONE BUNTS

THE MANAGER WHO WAS A COACH

Jim Serger

EVERYONE BUNTS

THE MANAGER WHO WAS A COACH

Jim Serger

Red Bike Publishing LLC
Huntsville, Alabama

Everyone Bunts

Published by: Red Bike Publishing, LLC

Published in the United States of America
https://www.redbikepublishing.com

Red Bike Publishing also publishes books in electronic format. Some publications appearing in print may not be available in electronic book format. Red Bike Publishing also publishes books in electronic format.
Picture designs by Craig Moore

Library of Congress Control Number: 2026933800
ISBN: 978-1-936800-56-8

EVERYONE BUNTS

THE MANAGER WHO WAS A COACH

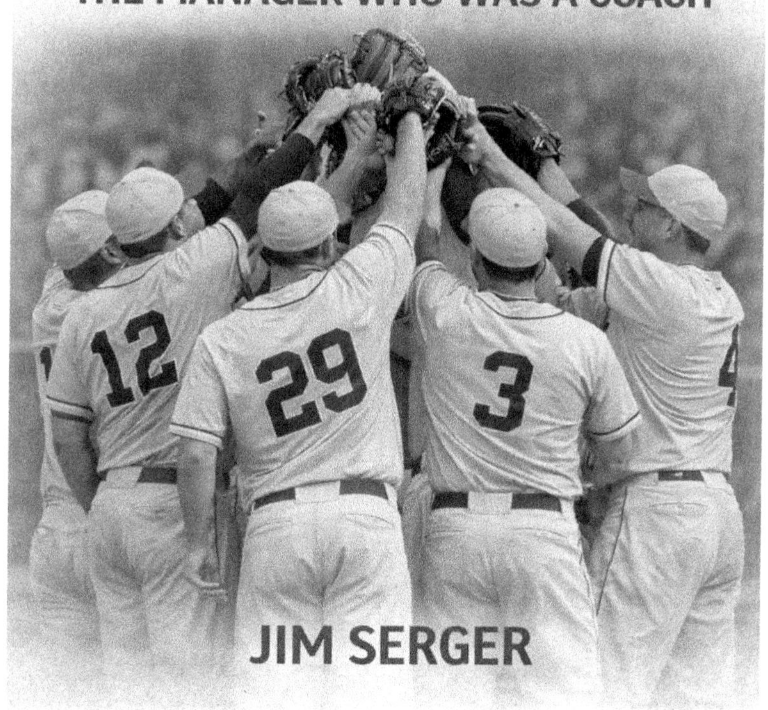

This book is dedicated to Gary Pierson—the greatest baseball coach, teacher, and mentor I ever had.

"Pop! Pop! Pop! That is the sound of life lessons being learned on the diamond. The hardest thing in life is to know when to *BUNT*."
~Jason Tice NAIA World Series Umpire

"*Everybody Bunts* is a must read. The story brought back so many memories of my high school days, the tryouts, the coaches, and the players. Especially Coach R— his influence on the kids, the culture and respecting each other and your opponents. TEAM was truly evident in this book. Serger's book in baseball terms is a "no-doubter", a true "dinger". As a big sports enthusiast I highly recommend reading this, it will take you back to your playing days!"
~Dan Albers Anderson High School Hall-of-Fame Inductee, President of *USBN Sports*

"Jim Serger, author of nine books including three in the '9:11 A Time To Always Remember' series returns with another inspirational book wrapped around his favorite pastime, baseball. A lifetime Cincinnati Reds fan, Serger hits a literary home run (pun intended) with his latest 'Everyone Bunts', offering up encouraging words from coaches who know how to motivate their players. Dedicated to one specific high school coach, 'Everyone Bunts' exemplifies the team (Together Everyone Achieves More) spirit. Including uplifting words from famed coaches such as John Wooden and Don Shula. Serger's new book transcends baseball and is a motivational game plan for how leaders on and off the field should interact with players, coaches, parents, business owners, and the community."
~Jeff Walker Entertainment Editor *Charleston.com*

"Jim has hit another one out of the park with his latest book! Be it coach, player, parent, umpire and beyond, this is a must-read/must-share for all! In a world desperately searching for leadership and values, you will discover each in *Everyone Bunts*. Jim cuts to the core of 'team' and passes on valuable lessons. From protective cups to changing tires, what a read!"
~Lance McAlister
Host "Sports Talk" *700 WLW*

"Serger's book makes us aware that a coach has to lead."
~Jerry Robinson
McNicholas High School Hall-of-Fame Inductee, D1 Baseball Player

"As a College Basketball Head Coach, I absolutely loved reading this book! Like any level from grade school to college, every coach would benefit from reading this book and learn from Coach R what it means to apart of a TEAM with lifelong lessons a coach can provide!! Even from my early playing days, reading this reminded me of old teammates & coaches who mattered the most growing up. TEAM effort from the coaches, players, scorebook keeper, & team manager...everyone plays an important part!!"
~Steve Ellis
Head Men's Basketball Coach UC Clermont College 2020 / 2024 National Coach of the Year

"Reading this book was like listening to a great baseball game play-by-play on the radio. Being a coach and umpiring over twenty-five years, I learn something new about the game every year. You can never know enough of the game—players need to understand academics are more important than the game of baseball. Without passing grades, the kids just can't play."

~Glenn Ewing

Mayor of New Richmond, Ohio—baseball coach for the New Richmond H.S. Lions

"*Everyone Bunts* is a home run! Jim Serger's easy-to-read writing style will encourage parents and coaches as well as the kids who play the game. Filled with humor and stories that will touch your heart, it is a book that will both entertain and inspire. Each chapter contains a nugget of wisdom that you can apply to your daily life. I highly recommend it!"

~Andrew Herdliska

Chief Marketing Officer, Orlando City Baseball Dreamers

EVERYONE BUNTS

THE MANAGER WHO WAS A COACH

"Great leaders have a heart for people. They take time for people. They view people as the bottom line, not as a tool to get to the bottom line."

~Pat Williams

Contents

Looking Back

"Well, there are three things that the average man thinks he can do better than anybody else. Build a fire, run a hotel, and manage a baseball team."

~Rocky Bridges

"Everyone Bunts!"

Those two words are how the new coach introduced himself to the potential players, at the very first practice in late February. It wasn't hello, nor was it good evening gentleman, it was hot off the press— "Everyone Bunts!" I can vividly remember that evening in the gymnasium, light snow falling outside, gym felt a little cold. Players pacing around the gym, at 7 p.m., on a school night—the first day of practice is always awkward, nothing is set in motion, other than report on time, bring a glove, wear sneakers, have a ball cap on, and be ready to go. Tryouts are tough, there are kids that have never played before, to those that have been groomed from the day they were born. Kids who have all the talent, to kids who have the biggest hearts. I have seen it all in my career, from the know it all, to the ones that haven't ever played high level organized ball, to the players who never practiced on their own, to those who go home, practice in their basements, watch instructional videos, and are 100% invested in creating a better outcome.

I have witnessed all the accolades that come from players' families—I have seen managers who carry that burden on the field, and it is reflected in their demeanor. It is just awful to watch. The coach, who wants so badly to watch kids grow and boom in this amazing sport, just get washed off and put out to sea by what happens to them outside of the lines of the field. One has to carry the tools to be both a manager and a coach, and that is what transpired the very first night of the baseball season, nearly four months ago.

It started as soon as I introduced him, "Okay guys, let's all circle around and welcome in the new coach, Coach Russell." With that Coach broke off from speaking with me and Coach Kuster, to walking up with a huge smile on his face, something the young men who have been around never had seen before—almost as if he was about to start off with a joke, as a matter of fact, in a way he did. Those words hit home with the kids, instantly taking center stage. EVERYONE BUNTS...

Not a peep was heard from the young men, a couple of neck turns, a few elbows to each other, but not one grunt, or oh man was heard from the corral of teenagers. "Guys I am Coach Russell, and I am a firm believer in the notion that we all are going to be in this together." Coach went on. “Success of this team, and of each and every one of us, will come from serving others. What I mean by that is the team is bigger than any individual here in the gym at this time, and that motto will carry us through the entire season.” The kids just looked at each other. The senior boys looked at the younger kids, and the younger ones, were locked in with precision attention—for the previous coach never spoke to them that way. “What is in the past is gone. We can never change the past, but we can focus on today, which will generate a superior future, both on and off the field.” Coach Kuster and I looked at each other, with an instant fist pumping under the belt wave—we knew over the years that this is what was missing from our team—the notion of putting others first, and that is why “Everyone Bunts” hit home with not only the kids, but with us coaches as well—it was so much exciting, that even Sweats, the team manager, watched with excitement on his face, and a head nod. He was instantly buying into what the coach was talking about. I am a firm believer that we get one chance to wow people, and back in February, Coach Russell hit the ball out of the park. He paced back and forth like General Patton and spoke as if he was at a TED talk—Coach Russell had the swagger legends are talked of—he even had a little Rodney Dangerfield in him, a few jokes to ease the kids. “Baseball is a team sport....no one position is greater than the other; the team depends on you to do your job. Shortstop, to right field, to back-up catcher, to the bullpen, to me, to all the coaches, to your mom and dad, even your brother and sisters are all on this team—T.E.A.M–Together Everyone Achieves More.”

Coach hunkered down on his message even more—it was amazing to see the young men dialing into what he was saying, for he was rooting for them, and it was on full display. How often do we see people out for themselves? Or the glory? Too often I would say. But there, in that moment, the gym lights radiating down, the hardwood floor glistening, the players eyes in complete focus, and I was right along with them. Scripting, watching videos, reading baseball books, studying player development—and many other things are all great assets to take on, to win. To win is more than just winning, its winning with ALL, and Coach

Russell was laying that vision out as clear as the blue sky right over the left field fence. We all could see his true personality taking over.

It was amazing. To share this tale, is one thing, to relive this story is just believable—it's what CEOs and leaders want to be a part of, what they aspire to be, and the sheer unconditional love of a team.... This story will hit home, because this needs to be shared from year to year, from player to player, and from coach to coach. Coach Russell is the nucleus we were looking for, not only for the team, but for my fellow coaches, umpires, staff, community, and our high school....

Everyone Bunts!! What exactly does that even mean? Secret to share, there were actually three words spoken—the third everyone had heard before—I'll get into that later.

Coach Eddie Logan Summer of 2026

Pregame

"A Coach must never forget that he is a leader and not merely a person with authority."

~John Wooden

It was right around 3:30 p.m., and the game was slated to start at 6:00 p.m. Coach Kuster and I were walking towards the field, carrying bags full of bats, and five-gallon buckets full of balls, when out of nowhere Keenan said, "Coach, let me help you guys with those." "Here, let me grab some too," said, Max. All season that was the tone, the tone of what can I do to help. Coach Russell, weeks back before the final game of the regular season, summed up the whole year on one word. MORE....in the final game we won 9-5, four pitchers were used to complete the game, two of which were our back-up catcher and our designated hitter. Coach Russell, put it like this, "MORE. We all did a little more than what was asked. We all did a little more than what was instructed, and we all cared more than we thought we could."

Coach pointed to every single one of us, including Sweats, myself and Coach Kuster and to all the parents waiting on the other side of the right field fence....We all did more, and in the moment walking to the field I saw firsthand why MORE was told over and over and over throughout the season.The kids were jacked up, proud of each other and they respected me, Coach K and Big R more than ever, in a season filled with ups and downs—but that is life. It's how we come out on the other side that will be remembered over time. This day the sun was shining, few clouds in the sky, high of 82 degrees, we could hear laughing by small children over near the park. We could see families engaging with one another—baseball is an amazing sport—when we all see the through the haze and the grey days, the running, the drills, the quick practices, the timely movements, that is what Coach Russell brought to us. He brought us together, made us closer, made us a unit. Big R, at the beginning of the season he was referred to as Coach Russell, but the kids out of respect, and out of the fondness for him gave him the name BIG R, as well as Kuster—the kids called him Coach K—and me, well I was known as Eddie...Ed...or coach. I looked back at the bus that dropped us off. The kids all had two items in their hands. Sweats even had two, just last year Sweats would have to make numerous trips to the bus, or the shed, or the locker room, but coach was adamant that ALL must be involved. No one is greater than the other—equal partners.

As we staged our dugout, Sweats could be a Marine, he could adapt and overcome any dilemma thrown his way; it was vision in his head, the layout of the equipment was perfect, he knew how to take charge of the scene and conducted himself as a leader. He was a trailblazer. The kids last year walked all over him. That was my fault, I should have intervened. I didn't. This year he walked with pride, because we all respected him. Hard to believe he has been doing this for four years, soon he will be off to college, and who knows maybe one day we will see him as a full-time MLB operations manager. Sweats' real name is Charlie Meyer, but the kids all know him as Sweats—he started working for the football team, then that led to basketball, and every time a player sweated on the court, Charlie would run out and wipe sweat up with a towel. Man this kid was lively, he was quick on his feet, beat the referees pointing his way. The student body loved it when Charlie came out. The spotlight was on him, thus creating the nickname SWEATS....

The diagram in his head was all set, and our dugout was ready to roll. Scorebook laid out, pen and pad laid out for the pitch count, water jug filled up, gum and sunflower seeds from the parents were all displayed in a neat and orderly fashion...and one thing that Coach Russell explained to Sweats that will stick with him forever is, "Plastics." Meaning have one plastic bag at the ready near the cups so the team can have a trash bag, so when we leave, we have this place cleaned up and in respectable presentation to the host teams operations.

Coach always explained to the kids, leave the dugout in better condition than when you first walked in—and all of us follow the golden rule. By the third game it wasn't a written rule, it was just part of our ritual....it was very impressive to see the kids in action—MORE truly is a fascinating word.... What can I do to help? How can I help you? What else do you need? As I looked around, Coach Russell was at home plate, looking over the rut always created by right-handed hitters. He was making sure the hole was filled in—something so simple yet overlooked by so many coaches. He always said as we entered an away field, "Check the right foot." Coach K and I knew what that meant–nearly every time it was acceptable, but sometimes it was a pothole. No twisted ankles today. The kids will create a new one, but let's always have a level playing field.... small stuff. He always knew what to look for.

That night in the gym, Big R gave me a whistle, and he said everything will come off your command—no one is in charge, only the whistle does the hollering...we do not yell anything at the kids in practice, we coach them, we explain to them, then we turn it over to the whistle. With that, I blew the whistle and the team huddled up right in front of the dugout bench. We were very early, considering the game wasn't for two and a half hours–all the players were gathered up, all eyes glued on Coach Russell–to this day, I can still remember the words out of his mouth, "Work together as a team. For days, weeks and months we have transformed into a unit of one, talk it up out there. Do your job. Think about the next play, and always with enthusiasm, cheer each other on. We have nothing else on our minds, the next nine innings belong to us, belong to each one of you–you know what to do Eddie. Let's go!!"

The whistle blew and outran the players and the coaches to their positions. Prior to each game we collected in left field, since we were the visitors today–the kids ran out, not a sprint, not a jog, but a speed that indicated hustle. It was a game type speed that others have seen over the years. Buckets of balls, resistance bands, you know the yellow, blue, green, and red—even weighted balls for soft toss were laid down.

The players all hunkered down on the soft grass, and our two team captains led them in calisthenics. "Loosey-Goosey boys. Loosey-Goosey!" Coach K would holler out using his fake bullhorn. Franky and Danny, had been selected by their peers nearly ninety days ago. Neither one of them wore a C on their sleeve, nor on the front of their jersey. Big R always believed that you don't have to have a title to be a leader–he felt that each one of the players was a leader both on the field and off the field–he always told the kids everyone is looking, everyone is watching. No matter if they know you or don't know you, you are a part of this community and people always talk–how you carry yourself, when no one is looking exemplifies your true character–so if you have the uniform on or not, you still represent this team, your teammates, your community, and your high school. He always had a word or two for the players, both individually and collectively. He never favored one or the other, sure he knew which kid had the best arm, the best speed, the best bat—but his style was like nothing I had ever seen. He extracted the best out of everyone, including me, and the other coaches–including, the biggest asset to his toolbox, the parents–he treated them all with respect. Knowing sometimes he took it on the chin, a whisper in his ear, or a pull to the side—he never wavered—he was who he was on the field and off the field.

Big R, Russell as I would refer to him, was thirty-seven-years-old, married to his high school sweetheart, and had three amazing kids–ages eleven, eight and five. His wife was a college cheerleader at the University of Kentucky, and he played college basketball, Division II in upstate New York at Daemen University. He transferred to Kentucky State where he started and earned his college degree in Sports Management. He grew up in Harrison County, Kentucky, even playing for the very school he is now coaching—Pond High, home of the Titans. He was second team All-State, first-team all-county, first-team all-conference, and was captain of the ball team.

Big R played football his freshman year, even played soccer all the way up through eighth grade—his dad would not let him play football till he was a freshman, thought he needed to grow into it, not just get shoved into it because of his size. Maybe that's why looking back, he never took an interest in the tall kids, like put him at first base, or the short stocky kid, with the exceptional arm—throw him behind the plate. Coach took it all in stride when placing the kids in the positions they were best at, based on their athletic ability. Not based on appearance. Russell's speaking abilities were to the point with the kids. He always explained why he did what he did—he always had a justifiable reason—even when he was in the wrong. He took the blame—from leaving a kid in too long on the mound, to not bunting with one out and a runner on second—he always took it, which made the kids playing capacity grow one-hundred-fold—he allowed the kids in the early stages, to think and react, not react then think. He told them all, being in the moment, trusting your gut, envisioning the play, seeing the ball—don't hold back.... I trust you.... Those three words, back in the gym in Mid-February, still ring true to these young men. TRUST is a huge word these days, and he said I trust you. I trust you to be smart, I trust you to be on time, I trust you to communicate with the coaches and me—That simple, yet effective tone struck a chord with all of us on those cold days. TRUST.

We were all gathered up in left field when the bus of the opposing team pulled up. Right away, Coach Russell gave me the nod, the whistle blew—stretching, jumping jacks, and sprints all came to an end—it was time to do a little catch. ALL the players did catch, even the pitchers and catchers—they never broke off for the bullpen. Big R thought that it was important to have the whole team together, to chat and strengthen our continuity. Kuster and I were chatting it up, going over a few key details for the upcoming game.

Coach K shared a story with me that he had told over and over and over. Coach K was on the Division I baseball team, down in Texas, at TCU. Coach K grew up as well here in Harrison County Kentucky—but he went to our rival school, Lakeshore High, home of the Stingers. We always played two games against them, one away and one home. That school was a 6A class, we used to be 6A back in the day here at Pond High, but are now in the classification of 5A. They were not in our conference, but both athletic directors knew the importance of continuing to play each other. Great for the community—football and basketball games were just packed, standing room only. Competition was always fierce, and all the players, including parents, knew each one on the other team.

"They know their ball down there in the Longhorn State," I said to Coach K— "It's small ball, that will win this game," he fired right back. I just gave him the thumbs up.

Small Ball... I had no idea what that was until he explained it to me and to the players back in February—in this moment, K gravitated to those two words, small ball.... Small Ball will win the game, when he first explained it to me, I had no clue whatsoever. All I knew of small ball, was a ping-pong-ball, or a lacrosse ball. I couldn't quite grasp what he was talking about. "It's the little things that win games. It's a bunt at the right time, it's hitting the cut-off-man in stride, it's the scooping of the baseball with a bare hand. That's small ball." Coach K told the team in the freezing gym....

The player's looked at him as if he were speaking Spanish, hola amigo, of course a handful of the players knew what he was referring to, including Coach Russell. But me, nope never heard of it. My background was a little knothole baseball as a kid, some soccer, ran a little track, but that was about it—what I was known for, was organizational skills—I was the high school play stage hand, the lighting guy, I was the guy who helped set up the gym for an assembly, and I was the guy who could rally the troops in a pep rally, loved every single thing about being around people. Being a part of the action was awesome, being in the action, not my cup of tea.

I was a hands-on math whiz, but an athlete, no way. The skills needed to plan an event were amazing, so years ago my kids played on this team, and sure enough the coach asked for some parents' involvement. I was all in, went from just here and there helping out to assistant coach, to dugout coach—I was the details guru, but it never came to fruition, there were always setbacks, nothing ever seemed to take hold. There was always something missing over the years with this team, finally the day had come where the previous coach took another personal job out of the state—so in searching for a new coach, Russell's name had been thrown out in meetings, and lo and behold he took the head manager job. I stuck with the dugout coach, that is my role, and I love it. Big R coaches third and Coach K at first.... of course, there is Charlie, I mean Sweats. He is up for anything...just an amazing kid. Hard to believe he will be gone next year. Who knows, this is a great job, he may realize that and is more than welcome back, even if he is in college.

4:30—down to an hour and half before go time. The other team was out in right field doing the pre-game warm up. I looked back and there was Big R about three quarters of the way over, walking towards the opposing team—but that was him. He was the team official greeter. He always said to me and the others, "Be the bigger man. Initiate the conversation, say a few words, introduce yourself before you meet at home plate—it's important to show respect to them. Even if we want to crush them on the field, we must extend an olive branch, to allow them to know we show respect, plus we get to turn a stranger into a friend—never know what will happen down the road. If we don't say hello, then we are just walking on eggshells and that doesn't help anyone." I looked back over my shoulder again, and Coach K had a firm handshake going on, and what looked to be a few laughs and a few congratulatory comments. It lasted all of five minutes, but it was the five minutes that labeled our team .... We are respectful, yet still going to play you head on...but first, let's do this. I could read his lips, "Good luck."

4:45—Big R gave me the nod. Whistle blow!!!! Kids ran right into the dugout, gathered up their gloves, gear and headed out to the field. I could not slug a fungo bat at all. I tried it back on our first outside practice and the kids just laughed and laughed. Even Kevin, our center fielder, did a better job. Sweats tried to give me a few pointers. Nothing was going, I did try my best, then I turned it over to Coach K. Big R loved to walk about the infield and talk with the kids, even floating out to the right field, it was something that was taught to him years ago, as a young athlete, and he felt that it still worked today. Encouragement, ritual words, repetition, a strict round of infield was always Coach K's strength. Man, that guy had a voice, "Let's get one." "Great job Bruno! Excellent job Franky!!" You could feel his excitement through his actions. It wasn't just motion after motion, it was action. Coach K was always feeling in his wheelhouse.

"Let's get two. Let's go to third." With a booming voice, K belted out.

"Look the ball in. Take a step." Man, this guy could coach. His fungo bat always making the right contact, and he even would joke around with the players. Showcasing his humorous and childish side–If I was an outsider looking in from the stands, I could see that Coach K had a presence to himself. A likable, yet terrifying glare to him–he stood six foot two and was about two hundred and twenty-five pounds. Could have been a middle linebacker at Penn State, linebacker U. "Coach K, let's do that again." You could hear the kids chat it up. Players were all talking, "Hit the cutoff man." "Move to your right! Here we go!" "Nice scoop! Nice rifle! Nice cannon! Excellent footwork!" You can feel the zest. And, of course, there was Big R—right there in the middle of it all. Thumbs up, double thumbs up... "Take your time, look the ball in...set up to make the throw." "Find the cutoff man and hit him in the chest." "Throw the ball, do not aim." Big R always had the right words, for the right moment. No matter the day, the time, the week, home or away–he was always himself. People say he is the team manager, but I say he is the team coach. Manager and Coach are two different things. Last season we had a manager. Looking out on the field I could see a coach—that was the difference. It was clear, as clear as could be. Right there, that day, Big R, understood how to turn it off and how to turn it on as the team top dog.

Looking back to last year, I could always sense that Coach Jones was not 100% invested in the team–too many little distractions to handle. We all could feel his temper floating on the field, as if he had a monkey on his shoulder constantly grabbing at him with all his problems. Coach Jones had a deep heart, but terrible management skills. He allowed everyone and everything to enter his brain and take over. Nearly every single day, a coach is inundated with hiccups, little speed bumps to slow the day down, that can take over the daily game plan. Big R, well he was different. He was the epicenter of the spiderweb. His head was always on swivel, yet when it was game time, practice time, parent time, or family time, that was centerstage for him. His memory was like a goldfish, he could instantly focus his attention on the team, without giving into the burden of the thoughts in his head. TEAM as he would put it.

Back in early March, the temperature outside was a cool fifty-two degrees, it was around 6:30 p.m. and practice had been going on for nearly thirty minutes. When out of nowhere came a parent. Not an everyday parent that loves to watch practice, but a parent who came up to the backstop and uttered, “Coach Russell, I need to see you now please!!” The whole team turned and looked and there was Colton’s dad—Like any response, everyone assumed that there had to be something wrong, and it needed immediate attention. Coach Russell ran over there and between the fences had a three second conversation. “Kuster, keep it going, I'll be back in a second.” Big R went through the chain link door, walked over to Colton’s dad, and the two walked behind the dugout—with that, not a single person could see the conversation being had, out of sight, out of mind. “Colton, let's get it home.” Coach yelled out, and practice resumed as quickly as you could say, can of corn. Nearly five minutes or so took place. Colton’s dad headed back to his car, and Russell proceeded to walk to the field...

“Everything okay?” I asked.

“Yes.” He countered, and followed up with, "I'll tell you later.”

Practice wrapped up at 7:30—Coach never believed in more than ninety-minute practices. As we walked out, Coach K and I were walking behind the kids. “Russ, what is going on with Colton’s dad?” We asked. He turned and I’ll never forget his response, “Not here, and not ever.” We both knew right away that we never have conversations, unless it's about baseball within an earshot of the kids.

As we said good-bye to the kids, the three of us circled up around Russ’ pick-up truck and he proceeded to tell us what had happened. We thought the worst but hoped for the best.

“Colton’s dad wanted to see if it was okay to have the team over to their house for a pizza party, that's it.”

“WHAT???” A look of bewilderment came over Coach K.

“That was it,” perplexed.

Big R in a nonchalant way. “Yes, but I told him he needs to follow the rules.”

The rules were simple that the coach had laid out in the gym nearly one hundred days ago. All parents are more than welcome to come to practice, but practice is the focus, unless there is a serious emergency, then of course interrupt, but nothing other than an emergency will be tolerated.

“I explained to Colton’s dad that this is a golden rule. We are only given so much time. We use that time wisely, to our advantage. Just five minutes can throw us off kilter all practice.”

“Now here is the deal,” he went on. “Notice how practice kept going, the kids were engaged, and when I came back to the field, Colton was looking right at me. I gave him a quick thumbs up, to reassure him everything was good to go.”

“Yes, I saw.”

“Me too.”

He continued with his insider trading information, “We never make anything a big deal with parents, with the kids, or anyone else. It’s not what we are here for. We are here to guide, understand and show compassion to others.”

Colton's dad, as small as it seems, thought the pizza party was a big deal. Which was very nice of him, but it was not so important to stop practice. After practice, never during, was hammered home. Managing his time and ours more fluidly—and with this, we hope other parents will get the drift. Kids first, everything else is secondary. The feel for the game is important, we get one crack at this. Our time is very valuable—and it showed in that moment. As did today, at the big game. A manager is one who is accountable for overseeing the whole unit, a coach is someone who is in charge of keeping the unit engaged, explaining the rules, helping people understand the mission and giving the tools to succeed. Russ was a manager/coach and we all looked up to him, including the parents.

I thoroughly enjoyed music, and that day, in that moment, I watched the kids with complete concentration whip the ball around the field. It was well organized, on point, with complete laser focus. The kids could feel it. Out of nowhere Big R said, "Let's keep this crazy train plowing forward. Full steam ahead!" Crazy train? What was he talking about? Sure enough, the background music at the ballpark was blaring Ozzy Osbourne. Coach could see and feel that passion, the will to win, and the strength of many converging into one, our team. Still to this day, I'll drive to work, Ozzy will be on the radio. Instantly, without rehearsing, that moment pops into my subconscious. Amazing little memory, that is stored forever. Powerful stuff.

Coach gave me the nod, the whistle blew, and the kids all ran into the dugout. It was time for the opposing team to take the field. Sweats was handing out cups of water like crazy.

"Looking good guys. Keep it up." I heard him say, and if Sweats is engaged, the flow of the day is looking amazing.

Big R took the pitchers over to the bullpen, and the catchers as well. Warm-up had started to commence. Coach K had the rest of the kids take five on the bench. I sat in the corner, and got out my blank line-up card and began to fill it in. Today each and every kid and coach knew their role. It was amazing to see this take a strong hold. Klaus, our starting pitcher, as well as Colton were down stretching and warming up, we were now down to about thirty-five minutes till game time. Big R was the best of the best, down at the bullpen, you could see his head peeking out over the fence and see a huge smile on his face—the face of a man who knew we were ready.

I remember back to the gym days, the very early stages of tryouts. Big R and Coach K were asking the kids who can throw as they stood on the fake wooden pitcher's mound—now for the record, Coach K and I knew who we had in mind to start. Colton of course. Big R had a different philosophy. He stood up in front of the players,

"Who here can throw a ball to home plate?" Instantly, nearly half of the kids stood up. "So, what you are telling me is that the other half can't throw a ball sixty feet, six inches...is that correct?"

Boom, like a spring, they all stood up. It was classic Big R, he didn't ask who was a pitcher, he just asked a simple question, who can throw a ball, which all the kids assumed it meant, who among you is a pitcher? Big R's philosophy was that pitchers are limited in that we all are going to be pitchers.

"We have to complete a game. In order to complete a game, we have to have pitchers." He continued, "Now, who can throw a ball over the plate?"

With that response about seven guys stepped forward and sure enough, those were the ones who could do it. The one person who did not step forward was Max, "HULK," as his friends would call him. He was our D.H. Stocky kid, basically looked like he could lift a car or bus over his head, but his precision throws made him an prime candidate for a relief pitcher.

"Max, get over here." Big R hollered out. "Let me see you throw to Kevin off this mound." "NOT HARD, just throw."

Max took his position on the turf wood pitching mound. Kevin took his spot behind the thin plastic fake home plate.

"Okay, let's see what you have. But not hard."

"Okay coach."

With a little awkward motion, Max took what appeared to be windup and threw the ball with half effort. It sailed right over the plate, into Kevin's glove.

"Strike one!" Coach K yelled out...

"Do it again." The ball exploded, with a massive pop in the catcher's mitt.

"Strike two. One more time."

"Yeah Coach." Max shaking his head, with a smirk for all to see.

"Strike three! Take your seat batter," Big R shared with the players.

All the players laughed. They laughed for two reasons. One—Max proved to everyone that he could throw the ball over the plate. Two—Max did something, for the first time, and was very proud of it. Kids are kids. They are going to laugh, but when Max came off the mound, a few of his buddies gave him a high-five and Big R grabbed him by the bill of the hat, shook it and said,

"See, we don't have to throw hard, to get the ball over the plate. Every single one of you will get the chance to do the same thing. Next Up!" Coach hollered, and before we knew it every single kid lined up to throw strikes ....

"Not hard. No Randy Johnson. Just throw the ball," Big R uttered.

It was amazing to watch, the kids all rallied around the drill, like I had never seen–they all were buying into the coach's concept of we are all in this together. Yes, Colton was our starting pitcher, but so was a young man named Klaus, and in that moment the coaches and I saw for the first time in years, players who normally stood their ground with a hard "NO", were now standing side-by-side showcasing to all that they were a "YES." Just awesome to watch. In that brief fifteen minutes, Big R proved to all that a comfort zone is just boring. You can't grow and gain new insight sitting on the sidelines. Now of course, there were a few that would never take the mound, which is fine—but never say never was front and center and it was amazing to witness the camaraderie formed in a quarter of an hour—kids were yelling, "Ball, strike, hit the batter, or just a bit outside." Unit of one philosophy was taking a stronghold, and the kids and I were having a blast. That is the essence of a great team—learning something new together and having a blast while doing so... Big R was proving that all of us have to do our part in order for the team to win, and small sacrifices like possibly pitching one inning, or so will take it to the next level.

“Throw strikes, that's all we have to do. Throw strikes,” Big R barreled out.

“What???? No curve balls, no sliders, no change ups,” Joey hollered out, with a grin on his face.

“Yes! When it is your call to the mound, throw strikes, no goofy, off the cuff stuff. I would rather a batter lambasted a moon shot, knowing you are throwing strikes, than have bases loaded on back-to-back-to- back walks—we will make the other team bat,” Big R barreled out.

Coach K second that notion. “Let our defense play.”

As our team hustled off the field, it was now 5:15. Once the whistle blew, all knew where to muster up and proceed with the next leg of the pre-game ritual. As for me, well I had to use my Marine Recon skills, in what Big R termed, “I spot with my little eye.” Coach would put it this way as we broke off, “Recon 101 Eddie. Recon 101.” With that I would head back into our dugout, grab my scorebook and begin my notes on the opposing team—now for the record, we had never, ever played this team before.

We didn’t know any of the coaches. Nor did our players know any of theirs. So, this was my chance to pick up on key words they were saying, key infielders’ motions, how the outfield played, and all the guys threw. It was very simple, always looking for the players actions, hustle, or lack thereof. If I can pick it up, I know the other team already knows the weakness of the players.

As I sat there, Big R said, “Listen to the coaches. Listen to what they are dishing out. Watch each player’s reactions to the coach's voice—head down, smile is gone, instant pouting.”

The game was an art form to Coach Russell, it was an everchanging evolution to what highs and lows can mean in an inning, or half an inning, he would explain that all the time to Coach K and me. It’s the little stuff that will work to either our advantage or to the other team's advantage. No one team at this level of playing is better at all positions than their opponent—it just comes down to reaction, strategic moves, perfect timing and looking out two to three batters ahead. Some days Coach R would ask Kuster and I out for coffee before the winter practices, and we would do a round table and evaluate every single player all the way down to the weakest point of each player–he taught us both the line rule.

The line rule is a very effective tool in evaluating players, you simply put the kids name at the top—what positions he could potentially play, and you create a line down the middle...Left side put Yes, and right side put no–then simply write down everything that stands out about that player—coach said, "KISS it." Meaning keep it simple stupid.... Sometimes what is overlooked ends up being the X factor we were looking for in the position player. So, as I sat there in the dugout, I would look over the key components to any team. Throwing, but not that simple, look for where the kid throws the ball, extremely high, or in the dirt—that is a key for extending a double into a triple, or rounding third and giving him the go signal for home.

"Why reinvent the wheel? Just stick with old school things that work," Big R threw out another round of inspiration to keep it simple.

I jotted down notes, not for an extended period of time, but just enough that we could get a feel for who we were playing–that was the key. Sweats and I would make sure the dugout was ready to go. The jackets were in place for the pitchers, and we had a first-aid kit at the ready.

The very first practice outside, back in March, Big R, made it one of his key components to have a first aid-kit at the ready–he always told the team and us coaches, "Always be prepared. Be a Boy Scout." Later I asked him if he was a Boy Scout, and of course he said, no. But the coach always had the right words to reel us in and pay attention and see things through.

He looked at Scott, our starting catcher in those early days on the field and said, "Do you wear contacts?"

"Yes, I do coach."

"Great, do you have any solution for your contacts?"

"No sir. We will only be here for about an hour and half, so no need."

Coach then came over to the plate, pointed at Scott and said, "I would like for you to stand in front of the plate, grab a handful of dirt." He pointed to Kevin,

"Kevin, I need you like you are sliding into home plate." With that Big R put on the catcher's mask, all the players were watching, eyes as big as cantaloupes.

Coach continued, "Scott, grab a handful of dirt, Kevin I need your feet about six inches short of the plate. Max throw me a ball when I say three. Scott, I would like for you to throw the dirt at the base of Kevin's feet.... okay here we go, 1, 2, 3." In an instant, dust was all over the place, Big R caught the underthrow from Max and a simulated slide was created for Scott to witness—Big R stood up and removed his mask–dirt, granules of sand and dust covered his mask, eyes, and head—

"Scott, what do you think? Should you have a contact solution."

"Based on that puff, yes, sir. I should have some." Scott stammered out, and the whole team just started to laugh. First-aid kit was always with us from that day forward.

"Boys, always be prepared." Coach R always made it important to teach the kids a lesson, each and every single day—not just for baseball, but in life, too. Here is another instant, real quick flashback before I get back to the game that was a complete home run for the kids–most of the boys were between the ages of sixteen and eighteen—so 100% could drive a car.

It was a galvanizing afternoon, in the early days of spring practice and one of the boys, Johnny, texted me and said he was going to be a little late. Extremely late to practice, is what it turned out to be. He was nearly forty minutes late and Big R never carried a phone while coaching. Kids came first. Johnny is running to the field like a bat out of hell—all the kids are pointing and Johnny hustles up. Coach Russell meets him at first base. A small conversation takes place, and Big R pointed right at me, and I blow the whistle. All the kids hustled in and huddled up around Big R.

"Guys, how many of you can change a tire?" Out of the twenty-five kids, one hand went up. Big R said, "Practice will take place at my pick-up truck for the next forty-five minutes.... gather up all your equipment. Get your cleats off and gym shoes on, the coaches will meet you all in the parking lot. Sweats, you too!!"

With that we cleared the field, making sure the field was in better shape than when we arrived. We all assembled out in the parking lot–car to car, and truck to truck, Big R went into how to change a tire on a vehicle. It was nothing I had ever witnessed before, out of the clear blue, baseball practice was canceled, and a life lesson took place.

Now for the record, I had changed a tire numerous times, but to watch Big R go into a classroom type setting and go car to car, was just awesome. Coach K and I were right there with him, each one of us took eight or so kids and went car to car—showing them where the spare tire is, how to use the jack, where to place the jack and how to pull off on the side of the road. We all became a very tight unit for forty-five minutes. To this day I can still recall how many compliments we got from the parents. Not only that, Big R showed a side of himself that was rare among managers, compassion for others. It was the rule—I am second, others are first. Coach K and I and the entire team vividly recount that day, when something off the cuff comes to us and needs addressed, we always say, "Flat Tire."

As I sat there in the dugout, I could feel and visualize the intensity of the opposing team. Great footwork, imposing arm speed, I could hear them chattering it up. But one thing that stood out in the ten minutes doing recon, was I kept hearing the word, NO.... Which was repeated quite a bit in the twenty minutes they were conducting infield.... Big R hated the word NO. It felt like a lazy way of saying you are doing it wrong. He never said, NO. He was a firm believer that if a coach was saying no, it meant he was not a stellar instructor for the basics needed to achieve greatness. In practice if he heard the word no, it meant an instant stop to the process. He felt that the kid needed more instruction, more guidance, a little more education when he felt it wasn't good—No always felt like pure laziness to Big R; he felt anyone can say no. It was an easy fall back for a coach, or anyone for that matter to say no. When In fact, he felt a yes always sounded better and was easier to handle.

Instead of calling out the kid in front of his peers with an instinctive "NO!!!" Yes, good footwork, nice slide to the right, nice step, but....... then he would fix the accuracy of the motion. It was far too easy to yell, NO–it took effort to say yes, nice job, good hustle. Instead let's try this motion and teach the kids. With that I was being taught how to confront kids with reassurance. Everything is fine. We can do this better–that is a leadership value. Use the setting to our advantage and conduct a teachable moment to the team. When you hear NO, time after time, it's a simple assessment that the coach is a manager–NO, simply means you are wrong.... Yes, indicates you're doing something right.... Big R always explained to Coach K and me that no means no. When in reality, we are just saying, hey this needs to be improved, and we can help you achieve that. No more NOs....it was that simple.

In that moment hearing the other coach said no, I knew something was not right, or just a little off. I carried that the whole season looking out from the dugout, it’s the biggest game of the season for these kids, and NO was used.... treat the young players with respect and everything will fall into place. It's amazing to witness and feel the vibe of our team, when watching others just do simple infield—KISS, keep it simple stupid. Baseball is not a complicated math algorithm. It's a kid’s game played by men. That's the key, have fun, work hard, be coachable, do your job and the end will work out fine.

I could see the umpires walking their way to the field—this was a big game, so four umpires were being used today. I could hear *Good Vibrations* by the Beach Boys playing over the P.A. system, and I heard the announcer say.

“The concession stands are now open folks. It's a beautiful day to play ball. Grab a cold drink, a burger or dog. Maybe even some popcorn and sit right back and enjoy some top-quality baseball.”

A huge smile came over my face. I knew it was time to blast the whistle, I stepped out through the chain link fence and blew the whistle one time—all the players walked up and as a team we walked into the dugout. Sweats had all the good stuff ready; blackout eye glare was laid out, cups of water were placed out. All the bats were neatly hung up and all the helmets were in order—Five brand new baseballs were by the corner of the dugout, just in case the home team had none to provide. Big R planned for everything. He even taught Sweats to have extra shoestrings and a few extra gloves at the ready, which Sweats had in his go-bag. Sweats even had beef jerky, a few cans of peanuts, and a few protein bars just in case the kids were hungry—Sweats was the Boy Scout now. Be prepared!!

"Hello Coach K, hello. It's me, Arnie's mom."

I could recognize that voice from anywhere. It had a specific ring to it. A nice soothing, high-pitch voice, that all of us, including the players could recognize on a voice recognition challenge.

"Coach K, here is the cooler of Gatorade for the kids."

"Thanks a million, we so very much appreciate your involvement." It was like something out of a *Hallmark* movie. That one mom, the mom who has her hands in everything–at least that was the way it was at the beginning of the season. "Coach K! Coach Russell! Coach Eddie!" Question after question, after recommendation—it was nonstop for weeks upon end.... Then there was the day, it all stopped. We were having practice on an extremely hot afternoon. So hot you could fry an egg on second base. Out of nowhere, a car pulled up through the **Staff Only** sign, turned around on the concrete and backed up the car to the back stop. Low and behold there was Arnie's mom.

"Coach K! Coach Eddie! Boys, I have some goodies."

Big R, just looked at us all, and practice came to a complete halt. Like seeing a meteor fly from the sky, it was electric to watch this parent. She was all in from the word go. The biggest heart in the world, always willing to do this and do that. She would round up funds from the parents for after-game meals. She would create a phone line with the players' parents. She was always bringing in snacks, she always gave off a Christmas season vibe, with contagious excitement. Even if it was spring time. That particular day, Big R pointed at Coach and me and said,

"Keep going. We won't stop the action...."

Big R walked through the chain-link door, proceeded to walk up to the car and pull out a cooler. He and Arnie's mom exchanged a few words. She pulled out and headed on her way. "Beep, Beep" was heard as she merged onto Oak Street.

"Boys come on over." Big R hollered over.

With that all of us headed into the dugout. Now it was blistering hot, I mean so hot that our mock turtlenecks were not even worn.

"Arnie, get over here please." Coach said, with a huge smile on his face.

"Open it up Big A." He pointed down to the cooler.

With that statement, a slow motion, reaction came over Arnie. It was as if he knew what was going to happen. He reached down, flipped open the top, and pulled out a popsicle. Laughter, and giggling took over the whole dugout from his buddies. Even all the coaches had a huge smile on their faces. It was an instant eyebrow raiser.

"Who wants purple?"

"Who wants red?"

"Who wants green?"

Wow, that two seconds of embarrassment for Arnie, turned into a story for the whole season. One for the ages. It was like Arnie was not even shocked. He knew this was going to happen. His mom had that touch of being involved–and at that very moment all the kids, and me included, were eating popsicles on a very hot day. It was a team moment, filled with laughter and brotherhood that just could not be explained. Arnie's mom wanted the team to know how much she loved the kids. It's a moment that you just cannot create on a whim, or even plan out—it's a timeless action of unselfishness towards the team.

"You have a green stain on your t-shirt." Kevin shared with Keenan, our shortstop. Keenan just laughed.

Here he was all decked out in his baseball practice attire, and lo and behold there were three green blotches in a continuous line straight down below his mouth. As I looked around, Keenan was not the only one. Stains were seen all over the place. It was contagious and after looking at the kids, I too had a stain of purple on my fingers. The tip of my turf shoes, you know the black ones with the white base–well the tip of the white now had a purple stain.

"Eat them up boys, make it quick. We need to get in one more drill, before we call it a day." Coach K shared.

"Scratch that drill and that drill. Time is important, and we will finish on time—so let's skip to the last drill." Big R told us, and we did. Ninety minutes was more than enough, and today as a unit eating popsicles, was no different.

I don't know the words that were exchanged between Arnie's mom and Big R that day, other than interrupting practice never happened again. It was as if it was a one and done from that day on. Arnie's mom never stopped bringing sunflower seeds, nor did any other parent stop bringing in gum, or any other necessity when playing baseball. It just seemed to be halted during practice, during the game. Four times were basically allotted, before practice or after practice. Before the game started or after the game was over—zero interruption was tolerated by Coach Russell.

Last year we had interruptions in all games. Parents would pull their kids over to the fence, give them sunflower seeds, hand them only water, or hand them only a pack of gum. Big R in the gym a month back, made it very clear we are ALL in this together. Everyone has to understand that no one is better than the other. If one person gets something, then we all get it. If one person strikes out, we all feel that. When we bang a round-tripper, we all feel that–not one person is higher than another. No parent is bigger than the other—everyone collectively has strengths that we all can learn from. Arnie's mom was no exception. I know it was hard on her to swivel from the old to the new. But as the season kicked off, Big R held everyone accountable, and collectively it was working. No interruptions whatsoever, ninety minutes is all we need. No more and no less—it was unbelievable to watch him in action. Which now was a reflection of me and Coach K–we were all sold on this... The kids loved it. Quick, fast paced and on point practices.... Parents loved it too—on time, every time. The Big R way.

As well hunkered down in the dugout, kids were pacing, double checking their gear, and chatting it up. A few pats on the backs, high-fives going around, Fist bumps too were seen. One thing that stood out to me was the fact we are a TEAM. Together everyone achieves more.

Lineup card

"It's hard to beat a team that sees something."

~Ray Lewis

Week after week, Big R always pumped ideas off Coach K and me—do you think we should lead off with this kid? Bat this kid fourth? Always hearing what each of us said. Taking into consideration how each kid did in practice, grew over the season, and which ones really accelerated on the field. Each player consistently knew their position, and a few of them were interchangeable.... right field to first base, catcher to pitcher, left field to short stop. Big R always stressed that our job as coaches was to watch the kids raise the bar individually, to see how each kid excelled at being adaptable. So, the very first practice out of the gym, we worked on the short stop drill. It was crazy to hear and watch this.

Big R said, "Every single kid on this team will play shortstop today."

Big R was told by Coach K and me where the majority of the kids were suited to play, and Big R took that under consideration. However, he looked at us both and said, "Shortstop drill will showcase each kid's athletic ability, from foot movement to arm strength, to maneuverability, to mobility and moreover, the fear of having a ball hit their way."

Coach K and I looked at each other, as if WOW!!! This is so simple, and easy.

Big R said, "Keep it simple guys. Keep it simple.... TIME, we only have so much, and we have to get the best out of everyone quickly and effectively."

"Everyone line up behind the shortstop!!"

Coach pointed at me; I blew the whistle.

"Danny, we need you at first base," Coach K hollered out.

All the rest of the kids took off and formed a horizontal line from second base out to right field. Big R grabbed his fungo bat and a bucket of balls–

"Coach K, you will be standing between first and second. Eddie you will be at third base—all we need to do is short to first, short to first. That is, it."

Danny hustled out to first. Coach K grabbed a bucket and placed it by first base ....

"Okay boys, all we are doing is short to first."

"But I don't know how to play shortstop," hollered Max.

“Max, no problem at all. It's simple, I bop the ball to you, you look it in and place a throw over to first base. Simple as that.”

“You got it, Coach,” Max hollered back over ....

Big R had a coachable voice. He never yelled, never screamed, never once did I hear him scold a kid.

“Okay, does everyone have their cups on?” Big R hollered out.

“Cup???? Stop.... wait...wait...wait...” Nearly all the boys ran over to the dugout and grabbed their cups.

“Boys, a cup is as basic as basic can be in this sport. We have got to protect our future,” Coach said. We all laughed.

“Here we go, let's get one.... look the ball in, take a small hop and throw the ball over. I do not want a rifle or a cannon over, it’s early in preseason, and this our first day. No Ozzy Smith tricks yet too. No Elly De La Cruz styles either—we are just doing a drill...this is not real time.”

“Let’s get one. Joey, you are up.”

With that, all the coaches began to see the athletic ability of each and every kid. Such an easy exercise, plus Coach was not hitting the ball hard at all. Look the ball in. Keep the ball in front of you. Take the hop, nice and easy...the drill was amazing to witness. Big R knew just by that simple drill, that we could start to pinpoint each kid's ability. The third kid up, who was an amazing hitter, was Max–he took his position at shortstop.

Coach hollered over, “Max, are you a welder or a catcher?”

“Neither coach. I am the designated hitter.”

“Super, then stop wearing your hat backwards.” Laughs like you never heard took over the infield.

“If you are a welder or a catcher, then you are cleared to wear your hat backwards. Until then, please wear your hat appropriately.”

“Yes sir, Coach,” players replied.

With that, nearly fifty percent of all the kids pulled their caps around and wore it like a ball cap.

Kevin was our star center fielder, and doing the short stop drill really showcased his speed, agility, and athletic motion. Bruno, who was the backup right fielder last season, was handling this drill really well.

Colton, one of our starting pitchers, was really loving this drill–as were all the players by the time we got through the first round.

“A little harder this time, boys. But still do not rifle it over. Not yet. Firm, but not 100% go time yet,” Coach asserted.

Now it was getting close to game time speed, close is the key word. A few bad hops, a few left and right movements and a few two bouncers were now being delivered to the boys—we were beginning to see potential positions these young men could play. It was so cool to watch.

One single exercise and we could visually see who could play where, just based on a half hour drill—the athletic ability was front and center. Simple task. Look the ball into the glove and throw it over to first... easy peasy...but like anything simple, complex was right over the horizon. When we think simple, we sometimes overthink it. We look for something collective to take with us, to look for something bigger, on a macro level. When in reality, it’s a micro level. Look down from 30,000 feet above and say this, react to that, yet when we hone in, look for that next puzzle piece that completes the right corner, that instant smile comes over us.

That day, the boys were smiling; Big R was not drilling the ball. He was not forcefully screaming at the kids, nor did he ever embarrass a kid. When it was Danny’s turn to slide over from first to shortstop, Max slid over to cover first for a while. Danny was as stiff as a board. No wonder he played first base–this kid was six foot two and maybe one hundred and ninety pounds...That first day on the field Big R gravitated to one thing Danny was doing wrong...Big R tapped the ball right to Danny, he didn’t even move. Danny scooped it up and threw it over to Max.

“Hold up a sec,” sounded Coach.

He left the batter’s box, walked up to Danny, and said, “Come with me. You and I are going to do a very simple drill. Ball flip.”

“Okay, Big R.”

“This is even easier than a slow-motion shortstop to first base drill.”

“Deal.” Danny stood there in a haze....as if he had never heard a coach doing a one-on-one drill with him before—which was true.

“Coach K, take over for me please. Danny lets go over to third base...”

Coach had two balls in his hands, and he asked Danny to drop his glove.

"Okay, Danny get in the ready position, and I am going to roll these to you, and you are going to catch them with your bare hands and flip it back to me."

"Sure thing," Danny exclaimed.

In a simple coach situation, Danny and Coach were doing ball flip—simply flip the ball to Danny, Danny catches it with his hands then flips it back to coach.

"Look the ball in. Don't think about it. Just react. Who cares if you drop it. Think of it as catching an egg. You don't want to crack it," Big R proclaimed, reassuredly.

In a matter of seconds, Danny's reaction time quickened. His confidence grew, and his oven mitt hands changed from blocks to butter. You could see he was making mistakes, but Coach was there guiding him through it.

"Next Up!" Coach K said, "Keenan come on over."

Keenan dropped his glove, and he began ball flipping with Danny.... the two of them were now engaged, having a blast, and in a baseball position, too. They looked at the ready.

"Next up! Colton come on over. Danny, I want you back at SS and let's pick up where we left off."

"YES SIR!!"

With that Danny stepped into the shortstop spot. Coach K took a poke at the bat, the ball took two bounces, right into Danny's glove. One hop, and Danny whisked the ball over to first base.

"Let's do it again Danny. Klaus over to ball flip."

Boom! Danny did it again, "Just look the ball in, use your right hand to slide in and grasp the ball cleanly. In a matter of minutes, Danny went from a stiff spruce tree to a very soggy french fry, able to see the drill front and center, and he was enjoying himself.

Magic. Magic just doesn't happen overnight. Sure, we watch *YouTube* videos, practice a card trick or two. Just because you can do one trick doesn't make you a magician. It just means you can do one trick—Coach was teaching these kids and Coach K and me, that the very simplest of repetition can create a magician. Magic itself is just a slight of hand, quicker than you are, a little smoke and mirrors—but life is about repetition if you want to get better, and it's recognizing that folks need pointers to get better.

Big R always said, "Today, we are better than we were yesterday, and yesterday we were better than we were the day before."

"Better takes a TEAM effort. We see something, we address it instantly. We don't push off until tomorrow, what we can address today...it's that simple." Big R addressed Coach K and I with that philosophy after each practice—he was a TODAY guy.

Close to game time, and it was fast approaching the bewitching hour. The grandstands were packed full of onlookers. Parents from both sides were up there, cheering their kids on. Children running around. The dads who hung out at the fence, were out there—with their faces planted firmly against it. The moms who brought their own chairs were firmly set up along the fences in right and left field.

It never changes, year after year—grandparents, and parents alike always have their own spot to watch a game. The one dad, who walks all over the field, well he is here, too. Baseball is an amazing sport, it truly is America's pastime—grandpas, dads, uncles, nephews, neighborhood kids have been playing it for years. Stories have been passed down from generation to generation, witnessing the growth of the game, to witnessing the growth of a community rallying around a team. It's special what baseball symbolizes. Baseball means spring is here, summer is right around the corner. It means winter is done. It means shorts, t-shirts, gym shoes and, of course, flip flops. It's the scent of a hotdog, the crack of the bat, the smell of freshly cut grass. It means kids will be playing outside soon. It means the world to so many.

Baseball is a funny sport. In that, backyard ball, all you need to do is throw, catch, and hit. Those are three essentials to having fun at the game. You don't have to be the best at all three. Just one is good enough to round up all your buddies and play a game of baseball. At the high school level, it takes discipline to create a winning team, a polished team—it's a tiny fraction that moves one team to the top, and one team to the bottom. Big R always reenforced the phrase, "It takes discipline to do the small stuff that no one else wants to do, to get the top of where everyone wants to be." Discipline is the very element we were missing, and Big R brought that to the Titans.

Franklin

LINE-UP CARD

TEAM Titans DATE 2026

	NO.	PLAYERS	POS
1	7	JOHNSON	SS
SUB			
2	55	Reeves	1B
SUB			
3	16	Green	2B
SUB			
4	44	Willis	3B
SUB			
5	17	TREAFOLD	C
SUB			
6	5	RIVERS	LF
SUB			
7	28	SNOW	CF
SUB			
8	77	VOGEL	RF
SUB			
9	99	Carlo	DH
SUB			
10			
SUB			
11			
SUB			

	NO.	PLAYERS	POS
12	35	ZAGNER	P
SUB			
13			
SUB			
14			
SUB			
15			
SUB			
16			
SUB			
17			
SUB			
18			
SUB			

NO.	PLAYERS	POS

MGR. Coach Russell

The umpires were gathering at home plate. Big R and the opposing coach were welcomed out to the ground rules meeting and exchanged line up cards. It's a ritual in baseball that has taken place since day one. Rules are rules, and they need to be followed. Big R had a paw for a hand. I kid you not. I believe if he and a bear faced off, Big R would win, claws or no claws. Big R could even palm a basketball. Once on a wild throw from a kid, he caught the ball with his bare hand. We all stood there and stared at him–it was as if this had happened numerous times, and it was no big deal.

"Good luck gentleman," the home plate umpire said and gave both coaches a tip of his cap—a little old school, but I loved it.

Normally head umpires are between the ages of thirty and fifty, today we had what looked like a sixty-year-old behind the plate. Old baseball values, tradition, love of the game—in that moment, I knew the head ump, home plate ump was here because he thoroughly enjoyed the game. He may not play the game anymore, but he is still part of the game. Once a kid, always a kid, we never let the old man in.

"Okay boys, let's go!" Big R pivoted from home plate and back to the dugout. You could feel his zest and passion in the moment. Then again, it could have been raining, with lightning all over the place and Big R still was upbeat and energetic...It's who he was. He jolted over to the dugout, grabbed a bag of sunflower seeds, poured a huge handful, and placed them in his back right pocket. A little bulge on his tail end...

"Boys, this is it. This is your moment. This is your time." Coach's head moving like a bobblehead, and his mouth moving at full speed. "You know what to do. Trust yourself. Your time is now. Today is the day." Coach always had insightful words.

I know somewhere along the way, a leader taught him those words. It was instinct for him to give a simple pep talk to all the kids. On que, as he wrapped up the talk, he would point to Sweats and say, "We are all in this together. Together we will make amazing memories. Let's make today memorable."

He would walk over to Coach K and me, shake our hands, and say, "Thank you. We have come this far, let's show our boys that all our hard work has paid off. Today is OUR day."

Big R always seemed to have the right words for the right moment. It was never staged or written on a little scrap piece of paper—it was real compassion coming from his voice box. We all could feel it.

Sweats always had two pieces of paper at the ready, first was the scorebook, nice and neat in the corner. The other was a simple white piece of paper on a clipboard, at the top said pitch count and the pitcher's name. Sweats was ready to go. Yes, Sweats was the team manager, and he was an enormous part of this fantastic team—all the boys treated him like he was part of the team from day one. Big R, at the first practice, summoned him out in front of all the kids and introduced him as one of the players. Big R made sure that his uniform number was #1—he felt that behind every great team, was a person who knew all the ins and outs of the program, kinda like a shoe-shine boy. He always seemed to know the scoop going on, just like on the streets, back in the day.

Sweats knew everyone, and everyone knew him. Coaches, parents, bus drivers, umpires, opposing team players in our local community. He even knew the grandparents on the other team. Sweats was our community liaison. He was thoroughly engaged. He was a lifeguard in the summer and worked at the local burger joint too, which was the hot spot for all the kids in the community. Sweats knew everyone. Hello Mr. Roberts. Hello Mrs. Merrill. Hello Mr. Truss. It would be like that all the time.

One time, we were headed home from an away game. Sixty miles away, when we pulled into a local diner after our big win, and out of nowhere two adults came up to our table.

"Sweats, Sweats—man, how are you?" They said, as one patted him on the back.

Right then, Sweats placed his napkin on the table, and stood up and shook both of their hands, and proceeded to introduce Big R, Coach K, and myself to this uncle and friend.

It's funny that day we all learned a lesson from Sweats. "Never shake hands with anyone while sitting down—very disrespectful." He shared with us, then said, his mom always told him, "No matter who someone is, whether we like them or not, we still show respect and stand up. We are always the bigger person."

Here was this teenage boy, sharing some insider trading information. A life lesson and a piece of wisdom for us to grow by. If his mom and dad would have seen this, they would have been so proud. But that is Sweats, part of this team and growing. Learning and sharing right along with us. What a heartfelt moment that was, that I remember to this day. I even have used that line a few times...Thanks Sweats.

"Five balls. Do we have them ready to go?" Big R pointed to the end of the dugout.

"Yes sir, we do!" Sweats reported back.

Big R always started with, "Okay boys, we know the drill. One half-inning at a time. That is all we focus on. Follow your gut. Pay attention to your coaches and listen." He would close it out with, "HAVE FUN!"

"If you would please stand, remove your caps and direct your eyes to center field, we will now play the National Anthem." Silence came over the park, you could hear a pin drop. As the last words were sung, "Play Ball' came out among the fans in the stands—everyone was excited to be here. The anticipation was electric.

Top of the 1st

"Success doesn't come from pie-in-the-sky thinking. It's the result of consciously doing something each day that will add to your overall excellence."

~Nick Saban

"Snap! Crackle and Pop!"

We could hear the other team's starting pitcher thumping the catcher's mitt—very crisp. A boom. Like a sledgehammer crushing concrete. We could hear it for a mile. I watched the pitcher warm up. Coach K and Big R would look at each other and give the nod, GAME ON!!! Instantly all three of us started clapping.

"We've got this, boys. We are all in," I stated

"Get your pitch. See the ball in. Hustle all day long. Hustle! Hustle! Hustle! Just like we have practiced and played a million times," Coach K chimed in. Big R ended with, "Let's manufacture some runs!"

We were scheduled to play twenty-five regular season games, of which sixteen were conference games. We had to get those in. Spring is a fickle season, sunny one minute, rain pouring the next—like Marines, we overcome and adjust. One weekend we had two double-headers to get in. I should have been a weatherman. I would lick my thumb and stick it in the air–then make the call for the day's game. Some days I feel I could have done a better job. Little spitting rain, turns into buckets. Overcast, turns into a scorcher–either way, some folks should have been farmers, others insurance salesmen. Myself, I should have been a weatherman.

I can instantly recall my heart was beating so fast with anticipation and with excitement. I felt as though I was back in little league again. As If I were the boy whose mom was bringing in all the ICEES from the concession stand. We were pumped. I had grape Big-League Chew between my cheek and gum, plus one of those small trial size bottles of water between my legs. Balancing the scorebook with both hands and reaching for my red and green pens–our color uniforms were red and black, so I always used red to pen our side of the scorebook, and all opposing teams were done in green. My high school colors were green—that way it was easy to flip back and forth—I truly was ambidextrous some days. Left hand and the right would flow naturally, with zero pushing one to outthink the other. Equal partners.

Coach K and Big R headed out to their positions. Coach K took his position as first base coach, and Big R was the third base coach. Sweats and I would handle the bench.

Our lead-off hitter was in the on-deck circle taking a few cracks as he watched the pitcher make the delivery to home.

"Second," the catcher screamed out and a quick around the horn. Pitcher and catcher were ready to go.

Big R looked in and hooted, "Let's go MARTY!!!!"

"Leading off, at shortstop, number seven, Keenan Johnson." The announcer with a cool, deep voice passed over the P.A. system.

Our bench was on their feet at the chain-link fence....

Marty you are saying, I thought the young man's name was Keenan. It is. Marty was the key word for lay it down....no signals at all from Big R into the batter's box. Keenan was quick and listened very well when developing his bunt. His hands were soft, a great candidate for leading off—last year Keenan batted sixth. What a difference a year makes.

"Ball, high!" Umpire shouted out. Even gave a hand motion. Leveling his hands up to this mask.

"Let's go kid! You've got this kid!" Our players were shouting.

The delivery was on the way, and Keenan, a left-handed batter slid his hand up the base of the bat towards the barrel. He squared around and drug the second pitch right down first base side...

"Go! Go! Go!" Coach K was hollering at first.

The ball was perfectly placed between the pitcher and first base, and about thirty-five feet from the batter's box. It was picturesque to watch this in motion. Dust flying up, the catcher was out, the pitcher moved over, and Keenan flew right down, ninety feet as fast as The Flash could have done it.

"Eat it, Eat it!!!!" You could hear the opposing coach, simply telling the pitcher do not even attempt to throw—just hold it. Get onto the next batter.

Man, that first notation into the scorebook looked so satisfying—

"Now batting, the first baseman, number fifty-five, Danny Reeves," the announcer hollered over.

Stepping away from the on-deck, into the batter's box, Danny peered down to third. "Let's go Danny, you've got this," Big R clapped.

Coach K was talking it up with Keenan at first and Big R placed his finger on his nose, then touched the bill of his hat. Danny looked down to third and Big R bent down and placed both of his hands on his knees—Danny instantly knew it was a hit and run.

Looking over, I noticed that the third baseman was three feet deep from third base and standing on the edge of the grass–the second baseman was in his regular spot, but the shortstop was about four feet closer to second than normal. The first baseman was on the bag, just in case a pick off play was asked for–sure enough my ESP kicked in.

"BACK!" Coach K yelled out.

Keenan slid back to first headfirst and reached his arm out.

"SAFE!" shouted out the ump.

Keenan stood up, looked over to Big R. Again, finger to nose, touched the bill of his hat and bent down to his knees—the same play was on.

The pitcher took to the stretch again. This time his left knee went past his waist, and Keenan was off to the races.

"Going!" The opposing squad shouted out.

The pitch was hammered by Danny right to the third baseman. He charged the ball, and knowing a steal was on—he fielded the ball, all the players on his team yelled out, "FIRST," and Danny was thrown out.

"One out!!!" All the players yelled out and held up the #1 sign.

I could tell right away this program was coached well. I could see this within ten minutes of the game starting. Keenan was on second.

The announcer went into, "Now batting, the second baseman, number sixteen, Joey Breen."

"Let's go Joey," I could hear his dad from a mile away. Mr. Breen was a big man and had a booming voice.

"Let's go Joey," he shouted again.

Joey stepped into the box. Big R tugged on his right ear, then brushed his chest, which simply meant hit away–hit away. Keenan took his lead and squared up the pitcher, shortstop and second baseman—

"BACK," hollered over Coach K. The second baseman, and shortstop were trying to do a pick off move, but the pitcher just balked it over. As to say, hey we know you are here, and we are too. The pitcher went back to his stretch and threw in a heater.

"Strike One!" the ump hollered.

Instantly we knew this kid had some game time heat—

"Okay Joey. Get ready buddy," and "Come on Kid," were coming from our dugout....

"Ball outside," blue shared.

It was a changeup, trying to get Joey to chase it. I looked over to the third baseman and he was really far off the bag, expecting that Joey wasn't quick enough on his bat swing to connect the ball so they were playing straight away—

"Strike two!"

Big R and K looked at me. I gave him the tip of the cap—which indicated Keenan is a green light for third.

Big R touched his nose. Keenan made eye contact. Joey was ready, the pitcher's motion was in route to home.

"Going!!!!!" The opposing side shouted. "Going!"

Joey had choked up on the bat, which created solid contact thus driving the ball up the middle. Keenan was barreling into third, when Big R waved him on to home—Joey was hustling down first base and made a wide turn to give a glimpse of him heading to second–Instantly I knew it was too wide. He slipped and fell...Hustling to his feet I could hear the ump say, "Out!" The center fielder made a great play, instead of frantically throwing the ball to home, because Keenan had a great jump, he heard "FIRST!" With a cannon for an arm, he nailed Joey at first.

So much was going on at once. What I did notice after the play at home, our next batter, Franky, had told Keenan to slide, that was teamwork in motion. 1-0 us, with two outs. Joey hustled back to the dugout, and the kids gave him high fives like crazy—he did his job, got an RBI. Like Coach K always told us—forget the mistake, I could tell Joey was crushed.

"Shake it off." I said, "1-0 us, because of your poke," and I pointed to the scoreboard in right field and down to my scorebook—it was classic.

"Now batting. The third baseman, number forty-four, Franky Willis," P.A. announcer shared with the fans—

Franky placed his right foot in the batter's box. Left foot still out, held up his hand for time from the ump and looked at Big R for the signal. Coach gave him the short, but sweet swing away motion. Franky took a few half practice cuts, and the pitch was on the way.

"Ball!" blue shared. Followed by a strike, then a ball, then a strike.

Franky stepped out and looked down at Big R—Coach gave him the double fist pumps with a big grin. Crack, deep to right center the ball sailed. Man, oh man–that right fielder had some wheels, which usually means he has an average arm–he caught the ball on the fly. Third out.

Kevin, our center fielder, grabbed Joey's hat and glove and ran out on the field–it was awesome to witness. Just last year, each kid was kind of on his own it seemed like—no leadership on the field, and no one had each other's backs–pretty selfish crew. This year we were selfless, watching other players' and coaches backs—we had each other's backs. On and off the field...Simple, the best to witness and be a part of. That's why I had to create this book. For so long it was all about me. ME,ME,ME—now it was about others, our team.

The TEAM mentality was flowing upstream, and like Big R said, "Only dead fish flow downstream." And we were not downstream at all, we were headed upstream.

"Excellent start boys!" A few pats on the back. "Trust your infielders, Klaus. Trust them." Big R reassured him that the seven behind him could play ball, and we trust each other. Klaus gave him the nod.

Bottom of the 1st

"Leadership is more about what you do. Not what you say."

~Derek Jeter

It was in our first real game of the season. Klaus had the mound, and he was bringing the heat—the bad part was it was like batting practice to the opposing team. Straight down the middle, belt high, the perfect pitch to drive—Big R requested time in the second inning and walked out to the mound. It was like a skit from a cartoon.

He gathered in all the infielders. "Klaus, this is Keenan, he plays short. This is Danny he plays first. Let me introduce you to Joey, he plays second and finally here is Franky, he plays third."

He asked Klaus to hold his right hand out and speared his finders. He did. "Klaus this is five infielders, and you are one of them— "Now make a fist. How many do you see now?"

Klaus smiled and said, "One powerful unit."

"Exactly! We now have a fist and no one can beat us. We are all in this together. Trust them to make the play, trust them when you are pitching, they have your back–that is the key, these four guys will protect you—allow them to effectively help you."

"Yes sir, I will."—sure enough, the game went as planned. All seven players behind Klaus were involved for the next eight innings–amazing.

Klaus took about five warm-up pitches and then Scott, our catcher hollered, "Two." With that the opposing player warming up in the circle approached home plate. The boys whisked the ball around the infield–hitting each other's chest with the ball. Just like Coach K and I worked on for weeks upon end back in the spring.

I can still envision the drill Coach K created—he learned this from his brother, who was a hunter. BULLSEYE—so one night Coach K came home and created a few XXL t-shirts with bullseyes painted on them. With that, each kid, while they were warming up and playing catch, had to wear a few t-shirts—not enough to go around, but the kids got their time in wearing the shirt.

Each one would throw to the target on the chest. "No aiming!! Just throw," Coach K always hammered down on the word aim....

Aim means we are thinking about what to do, and also thinking about the millions of things we don't want to do—like hitting Big R or Coach Eddie in the head. Never forgot that day. YES, indeed, Big R got hit in the head. It was awesome to see the kids laughing and understand the point of the exercise.... Lucky for us we had a crackable ice pack. Big R had a knot on him, and just kept on coaching. "Man, that hurt," he told K and me as we walked to the car after practice. He followed up with, "Work through the pain." We all laughed.

Two weeks later after initiating that rare and probably never heard of bullseye skit, he brought in another hilarious prop. This time he brought in a remote-control car. On top of the small sized 4x4 he had attached a simple cardboard cutout, and this was an all-out skit from *Saturday Night Live*. Each kid, while still in the gym was delivered a routine ground ball, then while Coach had the controls to the RC, he would act like it was stealing second base—then another kid was standing on second base simulating a steal, while still wearing his bullseye shirt and boom, one after another all the kids chimed in with the exercise—it was awesome....

It went so well that Kevin, our center fielder's dad, the next night asked, "Where is the new player? Ha-ha, I laughed—but that was it. Kevin's dad, not once had ever engaged in conversation with me or Coach K over the past few years—he was deemed, as I would say, a very busy man. Here on that day, at that moment, I fabricated a scene in my head around Kevin's dinner table—where he was sharing the RC story with his mom and dad and whole family. This image that you are having is an image that never took place over the previous years I coached baseball with the kids. Big R brought a side of baseball that was compelling, engaging, and darn right fun. Coach K and I were able to add value. Big R welcomed ideas with open arms, even if they were goofy.

The ball made its way back to the mound. Klaus was always told one thing, and one thing only, on the first pitch to start the game—throw it right down the middle. With expectations of the other coach doing a little scouting through the system, Big R told Franky to come in parallel to third base, not an inch further. Danny, too, at first was even with the bag—bunt was always on everyone's mind. Even the fans who followed baseball nearly always guessed bunt on the leadoff hitter. Shoot, it was just done twenty minutes ago. So why would this gang be any different?

As I peered out through the fence, I saw an upside-down V in the dirt at 1st, 2nd, shortstop, and 3rd—all four of them made that stance. Big R, while teaching kids how to get in a ready position, asked the kids if they knew a greater than sign, or a less than sign—

“Of course, we do,” blurted out Bruno.

“Okay smarty pants," said Big R. Then followed up with, “Let me see you draw a V in the dirt.”

“What...I ... .do not understand,” Bruno stood there bewildered.

“Deal.”

Big R stood in his ready position, with a table-top-back. Knees bent. Hands and glove in front of his knees. All ready to go. Coach then dropped his glove, and at that point created an upside-down V—

He said, “Boys, each one of you are built different, long arms, big torso, long legs, short, stocky, and some inseams are barely a twenty-seven and some I am sure are a thirty-six—so with that when you create an upside-down V, the tip is where your glove is, and at each of the ends is where your feet should be. The width of your stance, judged by your reach and build will determine the somewhat accurate account of where your feet should be placed—not too far off like doing the splits, or too narrow like you are on your tippy toes—but ballpark—that is a ready position.”

That day, and for months following, I could see all the boys as they took the field doing that exact motion–it was now routine. Before it was like Russian to them. Today it’s etched in stone and starts off every inning. It was awesome to see. The little things added up week after week.

“Remember boys, car wash stains are always welcome,” I said to all the players.

Car wash stains?? What the heck are those?? (I know you are asking.) Have you ever got a spot on your best dress shirt of salsa, or ketchup, or even a little grease on your slacks—and it just will not come out? Well, the same goes for uniform stains. From matted in grass stains, to crushed in dirt—white pants just seem to have a built-in magnet for huge stains. Sliding into second on a steal, to sliding back to the base headfirst. Sure, player’s brush the dirt off, but then Gatorade finds its way to the dirt. Then water and dirt meet, creating a little mud—the very stain that even Proctor and Gamble can't get out, all of sudden is visible. No matter how many times you try to wash them in a traditional washer.

After the first game of the regular season, Klaus' mom came up to Big R and was all embarrassed for her son. There, on Klaus' right knee was a very faint, but recognizable stain. Enough she knew the other boys would give him grief—and without hesitation, Big R said, "Car wash."

"Car wash???? What does that have to do with anything?" She stated, with a look of confusion.

"Easy! You know the clips at the car wash for floor mats?"

"Yes."

"Take Klaus' pants up there, clip them in, spray a little Shout on them, then power-wash the heck out of them."

The next game, Klaus' stains were all gone. His mom was the talk of the parents. Sometimes, you could hear her in the stands saying, "Car Wash Klaus. Car Wash."

From that moment on, all the parents were hitting up the local car wash with the stain situation, and boy oh boy did our uniforms glow, as if they had never been worn before—from our catcher to our shortstop, to even a dad who came over and told us, he got a grease stain out of his jeans because of the car wash—simple, yet effective. Big R the Coach, was now seen as the Manager. Handling small crises on and off the field—he was teaching everyone to shed the monkey. Shed the monkey is a term created by Ken Blanchard in his book, *The One Minute Manager Meets the Monkey*–where Ken shares how managers are always given monkeys, (problems) for them to fix. When in reality they can be addressed through thinking it through and trying to solve the issue themselves. Great book, I really recommend it.

"Bend the knees," Were always Big R's key words to the pitchers. It was just an instant reflex for him to spout off. If he noticed the pitcher was looking a little stiff—

"Bend the knees." Klaus, or whoever took the mound, knew instantly they were throwing with nearly all arm. Coach guided them on that principle way back in the gym. Here today, the old left-hander was on target with his pitches. Bending at the knees, following through with a smile on his face.

Like a whip striking on contact, his warm-up pitches could be heard, too. Piercing tone to it.

Klaus threw about 83 to 86 mph. Very good control, a few classic pitches in his arsenal—fastball, curve, changeup, and an occasional slider—but that pitch was tough for him. One thing he could do very well that Coach K and I coached him on was adjusting his speed. It was hard to transition from letting it rip, to taking your time. It was hard to tell a young kid, let it fly to slow it down and control the game. Through Big R's willingness and coaching skills, he taught Coach K and I how to think like a batter. Not to think like a pitcher—but see things through other people's eyes. That way we can keep them off balance. Anticipation is easy, but it's a ton harder if you have no clue as to what is coming your way.

Fastball!! No matter the batter, no matter the team, and no matter the pitcher of the day, he had to start the game off with a fastball right down the middle of the plate—two things Big R saw through this constant task. One, it gives confidence to the pitcher to throw a strike–and two, if the batter pounds it, the leadoff batter normally is not strong enough to bang one out of the park—well that philosophy seemed about right...

However, I will never forget playing the Springfield Knights for a second game. Same leadoff hitter as the first game, only this time Colton was the starter. The first game was Klaus. Same kid, this time on their field, and right down the middle went a fastball—Booooom, that ball sailed for an eternity. Home run, and Colton just looked at Big R as if to say, that batter had light tower power.

"It's okay. It's only one run," Coach said, then shared the next outing's first pitch. "Let's do it again in another week."

Colton just smiled, received another ball, and settled in. We won the game 5-2...the W is what Big R worked for. Not stats. Not the write-ups. Not the interviews, but the W. He knew the players were in it, to win it. That game, which seems like a century ago, showed all of us that coach was a believer in the system. A system that worked out till the very end—the system of I trust you, and you trust me.

"Strike one!" The umpire shouted out. "Ball outside," with a two-handed gesture, to wave it off to the left... "Strike two."

I looked out in the field and all the kids were itching to get one hit their way—everyone wants the ball to get hit to another player, just to get the elephant out of the room. But not today, our players were at the ready. Bring it, was clearly written on their faces. This time, the batter drove the ball to left center and Kevin was on it. Tracking it down, eye on the ball.

"Two hands," I called out, and like a hall-of-famer Kevin looked the ball in and clasped his other hand on top.

"One out!" The boys all yelled out and held up one finger.

We could not have scripted the first out any better. Hard hit ball, deep and a little left of center–butterflies I am sure came over everyone. The sound of the bat hitting the ball was solid, but he just didn't get enough of it. One out.

We always trusted our catcher Scott to make the right calls. In between innings as the game went on, Coach K and Big R and I would talk about the next batters up after going through the first cycle. My scorebook was like the Rosetta Stone. It was the baseball language to the coaches of how the opposing side hit the ball–was he left-handed? Right-handed? Did he walk? Was he aggressive? Was he a looker? Those things were talked over just a little between innings with Scott, who also pumped tactics with us. We were in tandem.

The second batter up, was a very tall and lanky kid. I knew Klaus would look over and he did–Coach K was on it, pointing to his knees. Meaning keep the ball down. Klaus took the windup and delivered a perfect fastball just below the batter's knees, his swing was so strong I think the trees out in left field even swayed back and forth to adjust themselves.

"Strike one," Ump pointed to his right and screeched out.

"Nice...Looking good.... play at first." Chimed in the team upon the next pitch.

This time Scott indicated a curve ball low and away. Sure, enough the batter chased it.

"Strike two."

Walking back to the rubber and looking in for the call—I could see no sign was given. Scott always knew what to muster up. He touched the top of his catcher's helmet. The pitch was delivered, and swooooosssshhhh.

“Strike three.” The umpire roared as his left arm went out and his right arm went back—this guy was 100% playing the role of the day, he was really into it.

Scott threw the ball down to third, and a swift around the horn whisked about.

“Two outs! Two outs!” The boys hollered out, and I gave up the peace sign. I mean two outs.

The next batter, you could tell instantly, was a ballplayer as he walked up to the plate; he batted left-handed. As he approached the box he gave Klaus a nod, out of respect for the game. Always love that kids respect each other on the field—on a grand scale I would label this kid as an instant All-American. I could see just in the pre-game, while he was out at second. He had that presence. He wasn’t loud, nor was he flashy. He looked the part of someone who was going to be in the big leagues one day. He was vivacious with his feet, anticipating the action. He seemed to devour the ball as it came his way. Not once did he struggle to get in position, and that is the key to an outstanding play.

Scott gave Klaus the call, one was put down. Scott also grabbed a little dirt, indicating to Klaus keep it very low—might be looking for the gas on the first pitch—the delivery was on the way and sure enough, this kid’s stance was very impressive—you could see his weight shift, hands perfectly still and slanted back, ready to shatter the ball—

“Ball down!” Ump shouted out.... pointing his fingers down to the ground.

Scott threw the ball back. Klaus took his look in. Scott called for a curveball, down and inside. The pitch, and boooommmm, there it goes. Quick hands in full motion. Drilling a line drive to right field, and I mean hard. A two bouncer just inside the foul line. We all could hear the rattle of the fence.

“OSCAR!” Our bench yelled out—

Full speed, this kid was fast. I mean fast. Bruno on his horse drifting back in an all-out sprint, he had zero time to catch the trajectory of the ball, he just knew the ball was going to strike the fence and he got himself set up. The batter was rounding first base, and Joey was on a dead out sprint to line up the throw to second, or possibly be the cutoff man for third.... Big R was looking at the third base coach and he was waving him on to third—

"Third!" Big R shouted. Klaus took up his position behind third base to prevent a pass ball, and potential score.

"Run!! Gooo, Goooo, Gooo!" The other bench was screaming out the dugout fence.

"Hit me! Hit me!" Joey shouted out at Bruno.

Bruno picked up the ball, made an amazing left turn and pegged Joey right in the chest.

Joey pivoted and made an amazing one bounce throw into third.

"Safe." The third base ump called. "Safe!"

Franky held the ball up and requested time. Time was given.

Bruno said, "Hey Joey, excellent throw over...."

"BRUNNNOOOO!! Nice job." Joey reciprocated.

It was a perfect play our team just made. In position, on que, and well-rehearsed—it was amazing to see this. Moreover, it was exciting to watch. Everyone in those thirty-five seconds was witnessing top-notch baseball at this age—you could feel the intensity, and I loved it.

Months ago, Coach K and I were walking onto the field, when Sweats was placing a trash can at the edge of the infield dirt, into right-center.

"What the heck is going on?" We said to each other.

Sure, enough Sweats just shrugged his shoulders, and came back in to gather up a bucket of balls and placed them at the pitcher's mound. Sweats then rolled out a safety net on wheels and placed that in between the pitcher's mound and second base.

"Boys, let's all head out to right field. This is one of my favorite drills," Big R shared with the team.

"We call it Oscar! For we all know who Oscar is, and how important the trash can is to him."

Big R grabbed his fungo bat, and said, "Okay boys we are trying to get a runner out at third. This trash can simulate the second baseman—we are all going to do this."

For the next fifteen minutes, kid after kid caught the ball on the fly, on a bounce, deep at the fence, or way off in the right field corner—Big R had precision placement, almost like he had GPS aerial support, or was using a laser to ping the location. But when you're good you are good.... One after another, crash, crash, crash, bong, ping, bang, bang—all the boys made their rounds. Coach K and I were asked who to place at second and who at third—

"Franky and Joey." We both said.

"Joey please take over for the can. Franky, please head over to third—Guys, let's watch the swivel, watch the arm release, and look to keep the ball down. Also watch how Franky straddles the bag." Big R gave the orders.

We walked over and Sweats was literally sweating–he hustled in and out, and before I could say a peep, the can and the net were off the field–

"Let's get three. Joey act like you are in position on this, watch it in and Franky will help guide and place you to line up the throw."

Crack.

"Three, Three!" The boys hollered and Max was the first one up ....

"Left Joey, left...right there." Franky guided him...

Joey headed out a little further into the grass, to the right. The ball was caught to Max's left, and he spun around, took his time, and hit Joey. Joey then spun and hit Franky on a line drive ....

"Perfect," Coach K hollered....

"Klaus and Colton get in here, question for you."

"Yes Coach," both ran in, and Big R pointed right at me.... Instantly I knew I had to address the pitchers—

"Where do you two go, when the ball is jacked deep, and a potential play is at third. Show me."

In a flash both boys took off, in a dead sprint about ten feet or so behind Franky at third....

"Perfect, we are all set.... Let's run it again. Everyone at their position...

"Scott, you are up next..."

"Yes sir, Coach."

Crack! Joey darted out. "Three, three," hollered all the boys.

Joey took his spot at the edge. "Right.... rigggghhhhtt.... perfect," exclaimed Franky.

Colton was sprinting over to back up third. Scott had to run all the way to deep right field, nearly in the corner, and without even coaching Joey scooted up about fifteen more feet. Scott hit him about waist high. Joey then swiveled and hit Franky on a one bounce ....

"OUT," called out Coach K. All the boys just laughed......

"Scott, get in here and take up your sport at home." I pointed to him.

"On it."

"Okay Kevin, you are up," Coach K stated..... this time it was a line drive. Two bounces—

"Right there. HOLD!" Franky said, and Joey threw the ball on a two bouncer, only this time the ball got past him ... Klaus backed him up, picked up the ball at the fence, and I yelled, "He is heading home."

Klaus lined up the throw. Scott was in position and on que all the players saw the play through perfectly from start to finish.

Oscar was now our call for the cut-off man in a situation, to take up his position. It was a fun day, and great to see such a silly routine turn into pure magic throughout the season. The boys and I loved the little simulations Big R would conjure up to make the practice more fun, engaging, and memorable. Big R always told Coach K and I, "Make it memorable and the kids will remember—make it boring and the kids will just fluff it off and act bored stiff." That's the way it was with Big R–taking a very hard situation, and miraculously turning it into something that all can relate to. Now for the record, half the kids forgot who Oscar was, but it came back in a jiffy when we referenced *Sesame Street*—then they all said, "Oh yeah, I remember that guy. The green dude in the can." It's exciting to witness men, still thinking and acting like kids.

Man on third and two outs....and the number four hitter was due up. Coach K looked out into the field and all the kids were even with the bags. A signal to the outfielders was given to take a few steps deeper....

"Keep everything in front of you!" Coach K loved that line—yet it was so true...

We never wanted to turn our backs, we always wanted eyes onto the field—always knowing what was in front of us. Klaus took the ball and took to the stretch. Scott gave him one and touched the top of his helmet–sure enough the kid was so eager to swing, the high cheese was foul tipped and walloped the backstop. Next pitch, Scott threw out the same signal, and this time he fouled back and out of the field. Next pitch,

Scott called for a fastball down and away—Klaus knew what he had to do. It was a perfect pitch. Scott had to slide to his right, and protect the ball from passing, and he did so–

"Ball!" The ump shared and threw both hands off to his right....

One and two, still a pitcher's count. Scott threw down another one. This time he hit the inside of his thigh. Klaus at the stretch made the delivery and the kid got a hold of it on the handle of the bat. The ball sailed to left field. A little looper and sure enough the runner scored. He got a hit—but it was a perfect pitch by Klaus. The kid just strong armed it.

"Two outs, play is at first or second," Joey hollered out.

"Let's go, you've got this kid." You could hear our bench giving Klaus reassurance, that was all good. It's okay. It's still zero to zero—with that the next batter was up, man on first and two outs—

"Focus on the batter," Coach K hollered.

At the stretch, Scott threw down a two, and smacked the right side of his leg. Meaning down and away...The pitch, it was a little slower than normal, but the kid was expecting a fastball and barely hit the ball, and Danny scooped it up at first. Klaus was in stride and caught the flipped ball, tagging first base with his right foot.

"OUT!" The first base umpire shouted.

Danny and Klaus gave each other high-fives with their gloves and all the boys hustled in. Amazing inning. Both ends. It was an amazing game, with great players on each side—so exhilarating, you could feel the kids in the zone.

"Quick on your feet, anticipate cover first base." Throughout the weeks, and game after game. Big R loved repetition, ingrained in the kids' heads—KISS, but have fun...Nothing so serious you lose all the kids attention. He was adamant about it. However, if it is called for, we address any situation instantly, just like we do on the field.

"Never push off to tomorrow, what we can accomplish today." That was my line, Coach K and I loved little snippets and quotes—movie references are the best. "You're killing me, Smalls." Most have been said a million times, as well as, "Wanna have a catch?" *The Sandlot* and *Field of Dreams*. Two baseball classics and all the boys had seen those quite a few times. Covering first, sounds easy from a pitcher's standpoint, even easier from a first baseman's standpoint. All he has to do is flip the ball.

We worked on this routine, time and time again...Over and over. From Max to Bruno, to Colton to Klaus—even Phillip, our relief pitcher and back-up catcher. I would round up the pitchers, and Danny, our first baseman, and I would stand on home plate—just me, and Sweats. He loved being included in drills. All the other kids would be off with Coach K and Big R conducting other drills–this one however, I just loved to conduct.

I'd have a glove on, the pitcher would take his spot on the mound, and I would go over the simple rules of the exercise. "Danny, this ball is far enough out of your reach, that you will have to flip the ball over to the pitcher. Or, for the pitcher if it's a bunt you will have to play the ball and throw to first. Let's go." I blew the whistle.

"No full throws. Just simple, work on foot placement, and on the flip," I would share with the kids–

Boom, right out of the gate, Klaus would throw the ball in. I would catch it, then throw the ball to the left of the first baseman. The pitcher then would take his angle, and take the flip from the player—simple,

Instantly, I'd voice, "Let's do it again."

Each pitcher got in about five rounds—it was quick. Took no longer that ten minutes. Once the boys had the routine down pat, I would throw them a curve ball. Pun intended, ha ha—sometimes I would just make myself laugh—because baseball is far from ordinary. Sometimes I would not throw the ball all the way to the first baseman. The pitcher then would have to react. We created two drills in one. As the season progressed, our practices were a well-oiled-machine—but it took time.

One day, Max took a great flip from Danny, but he ran right through the bag, and he and Sweats had a nice little collision on first base.

"Boys—inside of the bag–not outside. Remember there may be other runners on, so we need to be ready to make an athletic play. Plus, the key is, no injuries. No pulled muscles and do not run through the bag."

Reminders are easy, never once did I yell at a kid, nor did the other coaches.

"Anyone can yell, but not everyone can teach," Big R's words of wisdom to Coach K and me.

Top of the 2nd

"In baseball and in business, there are three types of people. Those who make it happen, those who watch it happen, and those who wonder what happened."

~Tommy Lasorda

“How many pitches was that for Klaus?” Coach K asked me.

“Sixteen.”

“That's great—keep it right around fifteen per inning, and we are good to go,” K sounded off.

He darted off to first base–and gave Scott a few words of encouragement as he was taking off his catcher's gear—

“Okay lads, zero to zero. First inning all over again.” Big R always told the boys when it was a tie, zero to zero was always shared. Letting the boys know we are in this, and we still have plenty of innings to go. One inning at a time. The opposing pitcher was popping it again. It was so loud; on one pitch it seemed as if it hit the side of a concrete wall.

“Now batting, the catcher, number seventeen, Scott Treafold.” The P.A. announcer chimed in right after *Thunderstruck* was aired. The fans get pumped up too, to a little AC/DC.

Scott always had respect for the other team's catcher. As he walked up to the batter's box, Scott would hit the catcher's shin guards with his bat and say a few words—this time he was not expecting this answer.

“Don’t do that again,” the catcher said to Scott, as he looked up at him from his squatted position.

“Deal.” Scott was quick—You could tell right away Scott was dumbfounded.

I was so thrilled this did not turn into a Brandon Phillips and Yadier Molina situation at the plate—fierce competition has a way of elevating tension–glad this was a one and done—no fight, no suspensions, no fines, and most importantly no one was hurt. Level heads prevailed.

Scott looked down to third base. Big R gave him the motion of swing away.

The previous inning, Scott sat next to me. He shared a glimpse of what was to be, “Every first pitch is low and in from this pitcher.” Scott was our #5 hitter this day, a very solid hitter as a matter of fact. We could always depend on Scott to give the ball a solid poke. This time I looked in and Scott's feet were a little closer to the mound than he normally stood, taking a few practice swings. The ump pointed to the pitcher.

He took his wind up, and the pitch—it was like slow motion as I remember, like a giant grapefruit was being walked in over sixty feet.

Scott shifted his weight back and smashed the ball. He ripped it right over the shortstop's head and into the gap of left center. Scott was built like a mini refrigerator, but still quick. He looked like Fred Flintstone dashing down to first, when Coach K gave him the signal for two—again, slow motion, yet his feet were moving so quickly. He walked into second with a stand-up two-bagger.

Max our DH, was sitting next to me, as he loved to do, and Bruno loved to do–I could always depend on those two lads to chat it up with me, double check my accuracy of the scorebook and offer me gum or sunflower seeds.

This time, Max looked right at me and said, "Look at the pitcher's head." I did, and he was staring right into the opposing team dugout.

"He looks like he let his teammates down."

"Yes, he does," I said.

"I am glad we don't have that problem on this team." He followed up with.

"Me too."

Now for the record, errors, home runs, misplays are going to happen. It's like life—it happens. But it is how we react to those problems that defines a person and a team.

Back in April, we had, let's just say, four errors in one inning. KISS was not working too well—the players felt it.

You could hear parents say, "Ohhhh man, he normally has that."

"Wow, I can't believe this is happening."

The one that hurt the most, and poor Colton heard it, was, "Take him out! Put someone else in."

Once Big R heard that last one, it was time for him to hit the mound. I still remember this well. He rounded up all the infielders and said a few words–never really knew what they were at the time. But while on the mound, I could hear "Yes." "Yes, him too." "Yes, that team did." Collectively, as an infield unit, all the boys began to smile, and a few pats on the back came around....

Walking back to the dugout, Big R turned and said, "We need one out, that's it.... go get it."

He hustled off the field, entered the dugout and pointed right at Johnny, “Have the Yankees ever made multiple errors in an inning?”

Johnny looked back and said, “Yyyyeessssssssss????”

“You got it. The best of the best make mistakes, and the best of the best gut it out and grind it out together.” Big R, clapping vigorously, shared with the whole dugout.

Next play was a dropped strike three. Scott scooted to his right, outside the foul line and made a perfect rifle down to Danny–third out and the inning was over.... After that game, Big R, Coach K, and I were sitting in the dugout, mauling over the victory of the day.

I asked Big R, "What took place out on the mound? How did you get the kids to forget it and focus in?”

He simply responded with, I questioned the kids, “Did Pete Rose ever make an error? Did Derek Jeter ever make an error? Did Will Clark ever make an error? They all looked at me kinda weird on that one. The point was hammered in–they all said yes.... Okay then, and I pointed, so have you, you, you, and you.” Big R always said to the kids, “Dump it! Go get the next one.”

Coach K and I laughed. Big R was right. Even the big leaguers produce errors and make mistakes. The great ones move on...What is done is done. Can’t change that. Can’t go back in time. Focus on the present, focus as a team and everything will work out just fine. Trust the system. Sure enough, we got the W that day. On a macro level we grew as a team that day.

One last item, which was greatly received—the agitation of parents and our fans settled down after that game. Anyone can coach from two spots. A lazy-boy chair and the bleachers. Folks witnessed firsthand that Big R and this team believed in each other, which then was felt among the players, players’ families, friends, community, and our high school. The Athletic Director was present that day, witnessing a coach be a leader and a manager who had to make tough decisions for the team. Win-Win and we got the WIN!!!!

“Now batting, the left fielder, #5 Arnold Rivers.” The P.A. announcer shared, as Arnie took his left-handed stance.

“Ball, high.” “Ball, low.” Blue voices.

"He's a looker." The opposing team's fans shouted out.

"Ball three."

Then the team itself shouted out, "He's a taker. He's a four-pitch walker."

Arnie never flinched a bit. He looked down to Big R and he gave him the swing away signal—Bam! That fastball exploded right off Arnie's bat and the second baseman was right there. One hop, looked over to second to see if Scott was going, then turned to first and threw over—

"Out!" The ump indicated.

"One down!" The infielders shouted out.

"Now batting, the center fielder, #28, Kevin Snow." P.A. announcer belted out.

"Let's go Kevin, drive him in." "Don't leave him stranded." A few fans gave their two cents—great stuff to hear.

Kevin looked up and it was his dad, and he gave him a wave. Kevin was the perfect student, always listening, always paying attention, always reaching to get an edge—and he always was the last one out of the batting cages.

Back in February all we could use were the pitching machines with those goofy yellow balls that just seemed out of place. In an indoor environment, they are easier to pick up with those huge, bulky gym lights baring down.

"Let me get in a few more coach." These were Kevin's words nearly every time he was about to leave the cage. Whether indoor or outdoor, he always asked for a few more—it just wasn't an I need attitude. You could see him working on his grip, and always asking the other players if he was gripping the bat too tight, stance too wide, lining up his knuckles correctly. Kevin was not the most gifted athlete by any means, but what he had, that exemplified with all of us, was a will to learn. The will to do more, and the will to give 100%. Most kids I have coached over the years had talent, but then again, most kids at this level have equal amounts of talent. It's what you do with that talent that pushes a person forward.

Some players are stagnant. Others are very dependable, but nothing more. Others surprise the heck out of you and that was Kevin from day one. You could tell he loved his parents, and his parents were so proud of him...Everyone knew Kevin's parents. Always there lending a hand, giving a ride, helping with anything. Kevin's folks were there. They were there genuinely. It wasn't forced, and his mom and dad always had the right words, for the right occasion. They never overstepped their boundaries, and Kevin was just like them.

I know what a coach is. We all know what a manager is—but to be both, to be given both titles, for one wants them both is what Big R, Coach Russell shared with me. Without ever telling me. He was the epicenter of the word nucleus. He was the linchpin that was missing all these years.

We were outside at the batting cages, and Big R was throwing the heat, well for him it was about 70 MPH. Kevin was the second to last to go, and practice was about to wrap up.

Kevin took his last two swings. "Next!" Big R said.

In came another kid. I watched Kevin step out of the cage and began to take some more swings. He looked at his feet, looked at his hands and made another few cuts.

"That's it, let's pick them up." Big R said, meaning everyone standing around, get into the cages and start picking up the balls.

"Coach, mind if I have a few more?" Kevin yelled over.

"Get in."

Big R walked right up to him, and they exchanged words—the next thing I witnessed was Kevin was over correcting his right foot as he unloaded to the pitcher. He was actually stepping left of the pitcher very slowly.

"Ready? Here we go."

Kevin took his stance. The ball was about knee high. Kevin took a simple swing, drilling the ball right up the middle, hitting the safety net.

"Nice. Again!" Big R said.... The pitch and whammo, once again Kevin drilled it at the net....

"One more."

"Here you go. This time full speed. "

"Yes, sir."

70 mph in. Kevin got a hold of it, and drove it right off the safety net pole, on a line drive. Indoors Coach K noticed Kevin was stepping to the

right, almost pulling himself out of the batter's box. Coach adjusted his feet with a few quarters on the ground. Kevin in his stance, stepped back, Coach K placed a quarter about sixteen inches up from his right foot,

"That is where you plant your foot." Since that day, Kevin's skills have grown tenfold.

"Strike one!" Blue shared.

Kevin's head looked in, and he looked over to Big R. Big R touched his chest, touched the top of his hat, and kicked his right foot forward.

"Foul ball." The first base umpire called out.

Kevin got a hold of one but pulled it foul. Foul with power is how I would explain it. Kevin was a lefty, always seemed a little afraid of the ball years back. These past months Kevin's batting average was hovering around .305—which is excellent for this young man. Just 365 days ago, he was somewhere around .225. His baseball athletic abilities were something you see in taller kids with a more athletic build. Kevin truly was the tree stump on our team.

"Ball, outside." Ump blared out.

Scott looked over to third, Big R gave him the sign. Sure enough it was the hit and run signal—only one out, and with a guy on second, we needed to move him over.

The pitcher looked back at Scott, the second baseman moved in and a throw over was initiated ....

"Safe!" The middle umpire yelled out.

Scott got up and dusted himself off. He looked over to Big R and the same sign was on. Scott took one more step for extra credit. The pitcher looked over, the motion was set, Scott took off.

"Going!!! Going!!!" The other team hollered.

Kevin looked the ball in, made contact and drove it right between second and first. Scott was given the wave by Big R and chucked right into home standing up.

Kevin made his way to first and Coach K was there to greet him and give him a pat on the back.

"RBI!!! Kevin, way to go!" Our bench hollered out.

The energy was back up, we were never a down in the dumps crew this year. Sure, we lost games. We lost games we should have won, but Big R always had an answer for that.

He once told the team a great Lou Holtz quote after we lost. "Ability is what you're capable of. Motivation determines what you do. Attitude determines how well you do it."

He always stressed a positive attitude, no matter the situation. Big R would always follow up with a *Young Frankenstein* quote, "It could be worse. It could be raining." All the kids would laugh, all of us coaches believed in each, and every single one of them—each one's ability was at the next level, or next levels: plural. It was fascinating to witness, even our weakest link from last year was now getting fluid amounts of playing time.

"One out. Play is at second or first." The other coach hollered out.

Kevin on first. The score was 2-1 us. Coach K gave the sign over to Big R. He took his ball cap off, brushed his hair over a few times, giving the signal that Kevin is going on the first pitch.

"Now batting, the right fielder, #77 Bruno Vogel." Announcer giving us all a 411, voice over.

Bruno, always had his head in the game. In practice and off the field—he was a five-star athlete, the cream of the crop—about six foot three and two hundred and twenty-five pounds. Our version of The Rock, "The Mountain," the kids called him, from the movie *Game of Thrones*. Just a massive human being. His mom played volleyball at Northwestern University and his dad played college football at Auburn, and even played pro football for the Chicago Bears. The Windy City is where his parents met. He didn't play too long, separated his shoulder making a tackle as inside linebacker. But, hey, he made it to the big time. It was in Bruno's blood. A gifted athlete. He loved basketball and football. He was a linebacker, just like his old man. The funny part was his older sister, Sarah, was given a full ride for softball to Oklahoma. His younger siblings were following in the athletic footsteps, too.

Bruno looked down to third base, got the take signal, which was simple. TAKE. Big R would pull both arms in, like he was taking something. The pitcher came to the stretch, Kevin's lead was a few steps bigger than normal, and as quick as I could see that.

"Back," Coach K hollered.

The pitcher made one heck of a throw.

"Out." First base umpire belted out–

With that play, the opposing team went into a frenzy. "Two outs!!!!! Let's go!!!!!!"

You could feel how proud the other team was. They should have been. The pickoff move went down, just like they rehearsed, I am sure over, and over. It was a cool sight to see. Strategy of motion, instantly became action. From a baseball standpoint it was fun to watch, from a team standpoint well that was not entertaining.

Kevin spirited on back to the dugout, the guys were right there to greet him. High-fives, and Sweats was right there with some H2O.

"Nice hit, Kevin." Sweats said, as he handed him a swig.

"Okay Bruno." Big R gave him the swing away sign.

"Ball high." Followed by, "Ball down," Blue shared.

Bruno looked for the next pitch, swung for the fences.

"Strike one." Umpire shared.

He was a little behind—Bruno stepped out and regrouped. Fans clapping, cheering and lots of excellent reassurance from our dugout to him.

"Come on kid, you've got this."

Bruno took his stance, and wiiifffff.

"Strike two—two and two." The umpire gave the indication, with two rabbit ears up in the air. He swiveled them around for all to see. This Ump was on it, a veteran to say the least—amazing instincts and great baseball characteristics from behind the plate.

Bruno took his practice cut, stepped in and right down the middle came a towering fastball. The very one we could hear during the pitcher's warm-ups.

POP! "Strike three." The ump went to his right, pulled back his right arm and threw out his left.

Inning was over—but we were up 2-1.

Bottom of the 2nd

"Practice is the most important thing we do. Because it shows up in the game."

~Marcus Freeman

“Be consistent. The results will follow.” Coach K told all the boys in the dugout.

It was his way of telling them all, nothing over the top. Keep it simple. Trust each other and we will come out on top.

Consistency is exactly what took us to the next level. Big R, in the early parts of the season, always seemed to guide us and walk us through situations that he knew would work out in the team's best interest.

Batting practice was the most tedious drill, Big R believed. He would clarify that batting practice never wins games. Our time was limited: limited on the number of days to practice. Limited with a short schedule to do round after round of batting practice. The early days, sure we get our swings in, but Big R cut that down—batting cages were meant to get your swings in. We knew who could see the ball well and who couldn’t. We would focus in on those who needed more attention. We did not tie up practice with all the kids on the field, standing around, shagging flyballs—boring as all be. Kids want action!

“Quick hands,” was Coach K’s love of baseball—he would demonstrate that in the cages, and he would demonstrate that on the field. His vision, early on, was that baseball is a hands game—the one with the best hands nearly always wins. He would always follow that up with quick feet and gut instinct.... Coach K always stressed to the kids, “Don’t overthink it, don’t complicate baseball—baseball is a kids sport, being played by grown men...." He loved that line.

Months ago, when we had our first outdoor practice on the field, Big R gathered all the kids and said, “Who can thump a four-bagger?”

Instantly, all the boys pointed to Max, “The Hulk” as they referred to him. Seemed as though nearly every kid and coach had a nickname, Hulk, The Mountain, Little Timmy, Big R, Sweats and on and on. Nicknames stick with kids forever, especially if it is a cool one.

“Okay guys BP will start in five minutes.” I blew the whistle.

Sweats got out the safety screen for the pitcher’s mound, and Coach K took to the mound.

“Max, you are up—swing away. Let’s see what you’ve got,” Big R clapped.

Max put on two batting gloves then took the spray pine tar can, doused his bat, put a little dab on his helmet—took a few practice swings....

"Coach K—let's see what this kid can do." Big R shouted out.

First pitch, poooowwww, right over the left field wall.

"Told you coach. Max can smack it...." All the kids chimed in.

I still can envision that day, Poooowwww, again right over the left field wall. Pooowwww again. Three times in a row—instantly I could tell Max was already getting winded. It takes a ton of effort to swing with power, and Max was doing everything he could to prove to his coaches that in fact, he could hit a bomb.

"Franky, out to third base please," Big R said. "Grab your glove and I'll meet you over there."

What Franky did not expect, was what was about to transpire.

"Danny, get over to first base please .... with all your gear."

Leading up to practice, Big R told Coach K and me that we were going to work on the unexpected....

"Arnie, grab a helmet and be a base runner on first. Joey, grab your gear and get out to second."

"Yes sir!" All the boys said.

"Okay kids—every single one of you get in your ready position, Arnie get a normal lead, with one extra step."

"Okay."

"Max, you've got this, swing away," Big R exclaimed.

Coach K made the pitch and whammmmo, another bomb to centerfield.

"Keenan, you are up." Big R pointed his way.

Now, what the infielders didn't know was that Big R and Keenan had a little conversation beforehand. Keenan took a few warm-up swings.

"Get in the ready position boys. Be ready," Big R said.

Coach K made the delivery, and Keenan squared around. He laid down the best bunt, right down the third base line.

"I thought this was batting practice," Franky blurted out,

Everyone laughed.

Big R went into his role, “Boys, no matter the hitter, no matter the inning, we have to be at the ready. Runner on first, possible sacrifice situation.”

“Yes, sir.”

“Max, get back in there.” This time, after he stepped into the box, I said, “You need to bunt.”

“But? I can't bunt.” A look of fear came over Max’s face.

“No problem. Just square up and bunt the best you can.”

“Deal!” Max with a half grin stepped in.

Coach K took his windup and threw it in, Max shifted his body, and got in the bunt position and it was fouled off.

“What the heck is going on?” Cried out Joey– “Max is the DH. Why is he bunting?” He went on—

“Great question Joey...Everyone huddle up.” Big R went on to explain, no matter the batter, no matter the inning, anticipate anything, think it through from your position and it will all work out fine.

“Boys this is small ball—anyone can hit. But not everyone can field, or cover, or bunt, or steal—this is us.”

“Next!” said Coach K.

For the next sixty minutes we worked on infield bunting and how to react to it—we put runners on third only, bases loaded, and runners on first and second. Coach K and I were explaining how to back up each base, and it was magical to witness.

A comment I heard from one of the boys walking back to their car was,

“What kind of practice was that?” He said to his buddy.

“I don't know, but I learned more today than all of last year.”

Learned more—that was my takeaway from that day, and the following months. Every single kid was learning, applying, growing, and it was the small stuff, it was small ball, and I was loving every single minute of it. We were not swinging for the fences, nor were we trying to throw 100 mph to batters. We were giving the boys the extras, just like a newsie would say, “EXTRA!! EXTRA!!—read all about it. Small ball wins the game.”

The sixth batter was due up. Klaus was looking solid during the warmups. "Take your time." I would always say to him. "No rushing," would always follow up.

This batter was left-handed, and the boys played it accordingly. First and second baseman always took an extra step back. Franky instantly took a few steps towards second and was dead even with the third base bag. Left fielder, a few steps closer to center. Center was in center, and the right fielder, Bruno, was a shade closer to right than normal—Klaus took to his wind up.

"Ball, outside!" Ump called it out.

"Strike one." Followed up.

On the third pitch what we worked on a million times came to fruition. He laid down the perfect bunt down third base line. It was hit a little harder than normal, but still just perfect—Franky reacted perfectly, and quickly on his feet approached the ball, picked it up with his bare hands and rifled it down to Danny at first.

Only this time it was airmailed over Danny's head–

The first base coach screamed, "Two! Two!!"

What neither the runner, nor the coach understood was Bruno had a cannon for an arm—a stinger missile with precise targeting, and was on his feet covering behind first base. The ball bounced off the fence and Bruno scooped it up. On a line drive, no hop, but with a beeline throw to Keenan standing over second base. The runner started to slide. The ball was there one second earlier and Keenan applied the tag—dust all over the place, like a mini tornado just went through.

"Out!" Yelled the umpire....

"Bruno! Nice arm." The kids threw comments his way. Bruno held up the number one finger, indicating one out.

"Let's run it again," I said, as I leaped off the bench, spilled water all over the place, and went into a deep, continuous clap.... I threw up a left uppercut too. For what I witnessed, was the old one two punch.

That is one of my favorite lines in practice--it means we are getting close to perfection, but we need to run it again, from the top. We must have run back up play after backup play nearly once a week when we could practice between games. Big R stressed to Coach K and me the importance of knowing how each player conducted himself at his position. Work on small stuff, so when it is game time, we are consistent on what took place in practice. Big R could not have been any clearer. Baseball I.Q. beats talent.

It was amazing to observe Bruno hit Keenan on a line drive. You get the feeling the sails in the opposing team's dugout just went flat. We took what was a great bunt into our first out, all because of small ball. It was the little things that created that out. It was rehearsing them over and over, embedding them, and explaining why we do this. Not one time in the regular season, did Bruno have a chance to make that play. That day, when it counted most, it came alive.

Up next was the seventh batter, their third baseman, a right-handed hitter.

"Strike one," yelled the ump.

"Ball one." Then it went into four consecutive foul balls.... good rips by the hitter, but also good location by Klaus.

"One more!" The kids threw out to Klaus.

"Ball in the dirt. Full count." Blue shared.

"Bring it!" Dugout shouted out.

Scott gave Klaus the signal for a curve ball down and away .... sure enough, it was way down and away. Passing by Scott and hitting the backstop fence.

"Ball four." The ump said and pointed down to first base.

First walk of the day, no big deal to us, our defense is solid. Up next was their version of The Mountain, their DH looked pretty solid, I would guess a two sport or even a three-sport player. Like always, Danny had a good hold on first, not this time Big R hollered out, "Straight away." Meaning play normal, do not hold the runner on.

Sure enough, as Klaus took to his stretch, the runner got a bigger lead, Danny hit his glove with his hands to let him know he was still present .... The delivery, and off to the races was the runner. Fastball high. Scott took the pitch and delivered a one hop to Joey.

"Safe!" The ump called out.

Last year if I looked out from the dugout, all I could see was Joey. This time if I took a picture, you would see Kevin in from center field, as well as Keenan scooting over from shortstop—all being a part of the play. Last year Joey was basically on his own, no backups at all, small ball at its finest.

“Aggressive Klaus,” I called out—reassuring him, it’s okay to throw strikes–always emphasizing it's okay to give up a hit to what most people think is a good hitter as DH. An awful infielder or outfielder—but good enough to swing the bat.

That is always the traditional thought of a DH, a stereotype. Sometimes we are wrong–might be a good pitcher or back-up catcher—never know. Labeling or judgment doesn’t do us any good. Like Big R says, “If you are on any team at this level, you are pretty good.”

Klaus threw another fastball, and it was ripped foul down the third baseline. 0-2 the umpire held up. Keenan and Joey were ready for a quick move, and sure enough Klaus spun around and rocketed over a nice throw–back headfirst was the runner.

“Safe.” Ump called out.

Scott threw down another one, indicating fastball. Klaus took his rest position and delivered a fastball a little over belt high. The batter made contact and drilled it to Keenan–runner on second was in motion. He then threw over to Franky, with a quick motion, a catch, and a swipe.

“Out.” Ump threw out.

Franky ran the ball into the mound and called time. “Two outs guys! Two outs.” Eight players threw up rabbit ears, “Two outs.’’

Once again, as always, fastball down the middle to the ninth batter, their left fielder. He batted left-handed, but threw right-handed–

“Coach Eddie, think this guy is a possible switch hitter?” Sammy asked me as he walked by to grab some Hubba Bubba gum.

“What gives you that idea?”

“Well, he throws right-handed, and now he is batting left-handed. I'd say he’s a switch hitter, bet you one bag of pickle flavored sunflower seeds.”

“Okay, you are on.” He barely took a swing, kind of half swing, like he was intimidated.

“Sammy, I think you are on to something.”

“Scott!” I said, he looked right at me from behind the plate. I gave him a repeated one after one sign—which meant fastball after fastball, no matter what.

“Foul ball.... Time.” Ump called.

Then he shrugged his shoulders and gave both sides the signal that his pouch was out. Sweats was on it—no more good balls, and he grabbed three from our secret back-up stash—gave them to the ump and darted off. Sweats was in the game.

“Ball high. Ball low.” Ump had a great eye .... “Foul ball. Foul ball.”

Sammy was right, it was not that natural of a swing. Still a swing, a compacted one.

“Full count,” Ump shared. Sure enough the last fastball was a little above the zone, and he chased after it. A protect the plate moment.

“Strike three.” Ump called out.

You could see Scott’s reaction behind the plate–he pointed right at Klaus as if to say, excellent placement and pitch. The boys hustled off the field, hitting gloves with high fives. All getting in the dugout and right there, you could hear a voice from behind our dugout.

“Nice job son.” Klaus’ Dad was right there to greet him. Not to embarrass Klaus, but another little pat on the back from dad goes a long way. Mom, too. When moms do it, it is funny. All the kids in the dugout always ride the player who was called out by mom, but when dad does it, it’s okay. If mom does it, “Momma’s boy.” They just laugh.

“Okay guys, one batter at a time.” Max you are up— “See the ball. Hit the ball!” Coach K said with a double fist pump, as he sprinted out to first base.

“Split the pot—50/50 chance to win it big. Hit the concession stands for a chance to help the baseball youth organization and a little pocket change to take home.” The P.A. voice blurted out, then he went into his sales pitch, “Brats and mets are a huge hit. Stop by and see us for a cold drink, too.” I just laughed. A little money every game helps out a ton down the road for high school sports.

Top of the 3rd

"Success isn't owned, it's leased. And rent is due every day."

~J.J. Watt

“Who are you? Who, Who, Who, Who—I really want to know.” That catchy tune was blaring throughout the ballpark speakers.

Now two things come to mind when I hear that song. One, do the kids even know who The Who are? Number two, that's the song from *The Masked Singer*....

Music and baseball go hand in hand, I always think it’s too bad we don’t have a real organ player at the park. Now that would be fun, but The Who song makes me laugh, everyone in the stands knows who they are, and all the kids in the dugout have seen *The Masked Singer*—I always say the quirky things about baseball, I just love it.

“Okay folks, we have a doozy of a game going on here—bottom of the third and leading off number ninety-nine, the designated hitter, Max Carlo.” The P.A. announcer introduces him.

Things are really beginning to settle down. Both teams are about to make their first go around in the lineup, nine up and nine down. Time for the next cycle.

For myself, I always seemed to make a few notes on each hitter and each infielder for both teams. On any given day, a star might not have the best A game, and a subpar player may outshine his teammates. Small tidbits are taken in by me and shared with Big R and Coach K as well as Scott, our catcher. After Max bats, I’ll call Scott over and mull over a few items for him to adjust for the next inning. That is always determined by how the inning starts off or goes—if we are in the zone. I do not even confront him—just wait till we retake the field—no reason to make him think about something that hasn’t even happened.

Big R stands down at third—their pitcher is still bringing it. Not as many pops as the first inning, but a few bursts were picked up. Clapping down at first, Coach K is giving the football false start signal. LOL—not really. It’s just a tumble of his hands, like a boxer on a speed bag, indicating to Max to get this inning started.

Max exits the on-deck circle and approaches the batter’s box—pitch count of the other pitcher is right at forty-one to start this inning—nothing too big. The pitcher has the build of a Randy Johnson, tall and thin, with one heck of an arm. Darn good slider and off-speed pitch, too.

Unlike Big R, the opposing coach allows his catcher and pitcher to dabble in the first pitch selection of the inning. Big R is keen on fastball, every inning to the first batter. Max takes a few cuts; pitcher has the ball, and it is still 2-1 us. Good defense, good selective hits, and everyone is in tune to the game. Even a few dads mustered up along the fences on left and right field to coach from a far. No game is complete unless dads huddle up and devise a road map to victory. It truly never ever fails.

Max takes his cut. It was a hanging curveball and he drove it to left field—one hopper and the fielder seized the ball, took a hop or two and rifled it into second base.

"That a boy kid—nice drive." Kids all bang the fence in the dugout.

Sweats even gave his two cents— "Max, awesome...." and continued with his onslaught of duties. He truly is the energizer bunny—he never stops. Keeps going and going. There truly is no bump on a log on our team. Coach K always shares his thoughts and ideas throughout the season, and Colton talks it up among the players. He repeats one of his favorite quotes, "Let's play two." An Ernie Banks quote from years ago—Coach K loves to say that, and it was perfect timing.

You could just feel the energy flowing out of the dugout. It was radioactive. We had a glow around us and in us, and we took it in stride.

"One batter at a time. One hit at a time. One inning at a time. One run at a time." Philip, while pacing the dugout called out, to reassure our team's motto, that was built in stone.

One pitch. One swing. One hit, and Max was out there. First, we had a single—Keenan was due up–approaching the batter's box with a smile on his face from ear to ear. If a family photographer were present, that is the picture they would have wanted. The game was fun, and in the moment, we were all having fun. Keenan looked the ball in.

"Strike one," Blue hollered.

As the first two innings were behind us, a little talk among the coaches always took place. What do you see? What do you hear? Instantly, Coach K said, "The catcher is basically lobbing the ball back to the pitcher after a pitch."

I chimed in, "When we don't have a big lead at first, the short stop is closer to third than in position to cover second on a steal."

Big R knew what to do. When the time was right.... Looking out of the dugout, Max on first and the lobs continued. I knew the time was right. Keenan looked down to Big R and he gave him the signal to swing away.

Coach K told Max, "Don't be a lobster."

Max received it through one ear and out the other. Gave the nod and stood off the bag just a hair—nothing fancy. Nothing to indicate he was going to steal, and there was zero pick-off move required.

The delivery was right down the middle. Keenan took a swing and whiffed.

"Strike two," the umpire called out.

As seen from afar, the catcher began to take his throw. All the infielders had their heads down, or looking off in the distance, and LOBSTER was in motion—Max took off for second base.

"He's going, he's going!!" Fans yelled out, and the ball almost like a soft ball pitch, landed in the vicinity of the pitcher.

Max at full speed was nearly three quarters of the way there. The second baseman and shortstop reacted like it was a chicken dance ceremony. Scurrying around and trying to get in position—Max now 90% there. Pitcher turned and hurled the ball way too high. Shortstop had to jump up and get it.

"Safe!" Yelled out the umpire. In position to make the call— "Safe!"

"0 and 2." The plate umpire yells out.

Our dugout was going nuts. So pumped that a simple observation turned into an evolution of trust, and the questionable play worked. That's why Big R always stressed to the kids, "Head in the game."

Max dusted himself off, and hollered over to Big R. "Car Wash."

Big R gave him a nod, with a grin and clapped his hands over and over.

Keenan looked in the next fastball in. Having choked up on the bat, he made contact and dribbled it to the pitcher. The pitcher was getting a ton of action this game, he snagged the ball, gave Max a look to hold him off and made a throw to first base.

"Out..." First base ump screeched out—

Max was held to second.

"One out."

Danny, in the warmup circle, was watching the inning unfold, and paying attention to the pitch cycle. He took his cuts, looked down to Big R–swing motion was indicated, and Danny took to the box.

"Strike one. Ball......Ball outside...Strike two." The ump called.

Terrific cuts by Danny, and it was 2 and 2. Umps hands in the air, giving shadow bunnies on the dirt. Danny choked up on the bat.

"Max you are running on contact." Big R threw motion words his way—Max took a slightly bigger lead—pitch was coming in and contact. This time it was off the end of the bat–literally, it was off the end. Excellent slider, but Danny made contact and gave a two bouncer to the second baseman. Who turned and threw the ball over to first.

"OUT!" Ump stated.

Coach K was right there to give Danny a high five. He moved Max over to third, into scoring position.

"Two outs!" The fielders hollered out. "Two outs!"

Joey was due up next—Big R stared him down, and again the swing away was given.

"Ball.... Ball...." Blue shared a fist and bunny ears for all to see.

Max on third doing a little log rolling down the foul line and cheering Joey on.

Joey took a step out and composed himself. Readjusting his batting gloves and his sleeve over his right elbow. He hunkered in and watched a pitch come screaming down the pipeline.

"Strike one," with a huge pop at the end.

Joey looked over at Big R—swing away again was indicated.

"Strike two." Joey took a cut, but pulled his head on an excellent change-up, something we had not seen thus far. Perfect timing. Two and two.

"Keep your head in," I hollered Joey's way–pitcher to his stretch, giving Max almost zero attention.

"The hitter! Get the hitter." The opposing coach blurted out.

He knew the game too. Two outs. Concentrate on the hitter. Max took a little bit bigger than normal lead and Joey got a hold of the ball, ripping it right down third base line, hitting Max in the leg—Max did his best jerk and sidestep, but it made contact.

“Foul ball.” Third base umpire shouted out.

“What? He was out.... he was in fair territory.” The pitcher said.

Third baseman also said he was out—then the umpire went right to the cleat marks indicating that Max never was in fair ground. All the spike marks were in foul territory. They both understood.

Simple fundamentals, had Max been in fair territory—third out.... Basics. It’s all basics and for months the kids understood right there and then...It had never happened before, nor had they ever seen anyone hit on third. Well today they did, and they appreciated Coach K and I going over that for months. Coach John Wooden would have been proud, fundamentals.

Joey now had a full count—I could see the pitcher was a little irritated at the last play and instantly he got the ball, took a short look in and was quick with his delivery—zero bending of the knee and his back was straight as an arrow.

“Ball four.” Ump expressed.

“Coach K. Let’s go Blue Devils.” Big R looked to the dugout and clapped his hands. The Krzyzewski play was called out. Sure, our team was the Titans, but during a game no one really remembers that.

Coach K heard it. Joey in a dead out hustle down to first was looking right at Coach K—Coach gave him the finger point and Joey took an all-out burst, made the turn at first and darted for second base.

“He’s going! He’s going!” Fans and opposing dugout screamed out.

The pitcher had no clue what was going on. Was it Max on third going? Who was going? Second baseman was caught off guard.

Big R was keen on taking advantage of a questionable play, and to use the momentum to our advantage. Joey was over seventy-five percent to second base; the umpire was not even in position. The pitcher threw over to second.

Once the ball was released, Big R said, “Go Max!! Go!!!!”

A huge dust cloud again was kicked up at second by Joey's headfirst slide. Something we didn’t like, but he was good at it.

“Safe!!” The ump screeched out....

Our dugout was going crazy.

You could hear fans howling, “Throw home.” “Throw to second.” “Hold the ball.” None of it mattered. Max was flying down the path and slid into home. There too, was a dust bowl .... but no play at the plate. Run scored, two outs and we had a runner on second base.

Max jumped up after the slide, and gave a huge double clap...the fans were standing too, cheering as well—at least our side was.

“Excellent job, Max.” The boys were saying to him. I gave him a pretty good hit on the shoulder—harder than normal. Max just looked at me, gave me a smile and a left-handed thumbs up.... adrenaline was at an all-time high.

“Joey!!” Big R shouted over. “Great hustle young man,” and tapped the side of his ball cap—without saying it, it was the indication of, be smart.

In other words, be in the moment. Don’t get caught watching the paint dry. Be present. Joey gave the nod. Franky was up next, 3 to 1 us, two outs and a runner on second....

Franky dug his right foot in, gave a few half cuts to the pitcher–he took his stretch.

“Ball high,” Ump went into a horizontal hand and gave it at mask level... “Ball two–inside.” Ump took two hands and gave a sweeping motion to his left.

“Relax. Relax. Bend. Throw the ball.” The opposing coach hollered out.

“Foul ball.” 2 and 1— “Strike two!” Ump pointed to his right. “Foul ball!!!” Ump shared and threw another ball out to the pitcher.

Franky stepped out, grabbed the bat with two hands. One at each end and hoisted it over his shoulder for a quick stretch–he dug in and the pitch was on the way.

“I got it! I got it!” Yelled out the first baseman...about ten feet deep off first base, and in foul territory he made the third out.

Everyone was on cloud nine–coaches made their way in. Big R stated, “Nice inning boys. Nice inning. 3-1 us, but we have a long way to go. Be smart. Talk it up. Have each other's backs.”

Kids took the field—

“Klaus...Klaus.” I pulled him aside. Remember there are eight guys out there, you make nine—they have your back, trust the system.”

“Yes sir, Eddie!” He took the field and made his way to the mound.

Still hustling out there. Like the game had just started. That's what we like to see.

Sweats took his seat between Coach K and me and muttered the words, “Just amazing!” Here was Sweats, ringing in the last inning with us both, and enjoying himself too—now this was fun.

Bottom of the 3rd

"A life is not important except in the impact it has on other lives."

~Jackie Robinson

Big R always stood at the end of the dugout, and would just crush those sunflower seeds, constantly refilling his back right pocket. If you looked down at his feet at third, or at the edge of the dugout, there would be enough uncracked shells to fill up a new bag by the end of the game. He was like a cardinal on a cold winter day, as if he had not eaten in months...

"Good job, Dad." I looked over, there was his oldest boy, Zack, peering up between the chain-link. Looking up to his dad with admiration—a father/son moment. Zack's eyes scanned over the field, and I'll never forget what he said to his dad, "One inning at a time."

That made me smile. Coach was more than a coach. He was a teacher, and his wisdom radiated on the field, but that little slugger looking up to his pops, mimicking the very statement he pressed on to us—coach wasn't just talking the talk, he was the definition of walking the walk. His son felt that at home, too.

"How many pitches has Klaus thrown?" Coach K asked the boys.

"Forty-four!!... Yes, forty-four," said Juan with an instant reaction.

Coach K gave him a wink, and a typical head nod, as if to say way to keep your head in the game. Juan was the twenty-fifth player picked up on our roster. Twenty-four seems like a ton. Going into that first practice of the season we were only looking for twenty-three boys—that is more than enough to fill a ball club, and Juan still had some growing to do. In the MLB draft, the last pick is known as Mr. Irrelevant.

That night in February, Big R, Coach K, and I knew right away that this young man was lagging in all departments. From speed, to hands, to overall awareness—we could just see he would not make this team.

"Twenty-three men is all we need to put together a winning program," Big R said to us as we watched the kids run laps around the gym.

Juan was never last. But he was never first, is all I could say. His feet were awkward, his throws were more like lobs.

"Just two more guys. Just two more." Juan shouted out, as all the potential players were running laps around the gym. He was a line leader. Now, to be fair, he was by far the youngest to try out. He was only fifteen, turning sixteen in mid-March, but his voice carried.

“That kid has some pipes on him,” Coach K said, and instantly invited Klaus over to the corner where we were standing.

“Klaus, what do you know about Juan?”

In a flash, Klaus said that a few of the other kids recommended Juan tryout. A handful of players noticed Juan always had a knack for statistics and was a huge military history junkie...plus his older cousin played college baseball, and some AA ball. He was currently in AAA with the Orioles.

I’ll never forget Big R beckoned Juan over once the laps were done. Sweats was handing out cups of water, and Juan sprinted over, nearly tripping over his own feet.

“Juan, if a man was on first, with one out, what call would you give to the hitter?”

“What number in the lineup is up coach?”

“Number eight batter.”

“What inning are we in?”

“Third.”

“Are we up or are we losing?”

“Three to one, us.”

“What did our batter do last time?”

“It was no balls and two strikes, but he got hit by the pitch.”

“Great, then I would allow him to swing away.”

“Why swing away?” Big R volleyed back—

“Well, the kid is probably furious, and frustrated that he didn't make contact with the ball—and the pitcher probably felt bad hitting him unintentionally—so this time the pitcher will try harder to place the ball, and our hitter will definitely make contact.”

“Dismissed Juan.” Big R said–

Coach K instantly said, “We have to keep this kid.”

Our trio, without a doubt, gave Juan a passing grade. We agreed he would be our twenty-fourth player.

I said, “Attention to detail. The small stuff...that is the making of a future CEO or Four-Star General...” We all laughed, and we all agreed.

We never cut anyone from the team, however, a few were sent down to JV. Seniors, well, Big R kept them. Not many, just a few staters. He felt it was important for seniors to be kept. A good way to finish out high school—part of something greater, a team. Create a positive memory upon graduation, instead of a negative one.

Forty-four pitches was not that much through two innings, but we were going into the third now.

"Bend the knees, bend the knees." I blurted out......

"Second base," Scott howled out...and with that the bottom of the third was about to commence.

Klaus investigated the dugout; Big R pointed down at his knees. Now between innings, Big R had a conversation with me about how to approach the next round of batters—he looked over the scorebook with a fine-tooth comb, and with a magnifying glass, as if we were about to storm the castle.

My notes were in order, and he called over Scott, before heading out to home plate. "High fastballs, high—on the first batter."

Klaus focused in. Scott gave him the one down and touched the top of his helmet. This batter's first at bat, he hit a drive to center field. Hit hard, made great contact. So Big R knew he would be chasing after the fastball—sure enough.

"Strike one." Ump called out.

The torque of the swing was as if he were chasing after the first pitch—but Big R outsmarted the other coach. Fastball down the middle is always the first pitch. Adjustments were made and it paid off.

"Strike two." Wiff again, man oh man this kid was looking for fastball down the pipe.

Klaus looked in again, Scott again one down, touched the top of the helmet.

"Foul ball." Ump held up 0 and 2 and rotated around like a Christmas mannequin plugged in—showing the count to both dugouts.

Scott now knew what to do. He put down the one and hit the outside of his leg. Klaus delivered the pitch down and away. Batter chased the ball, almost nearly throwing his bat to stay alive. Scott turned his glove backwaters and held on to it.

"Strike three." The Ump held his left arm out, and right arm in movement.

“One out! One out!” The infield gave up the number one signal for all to see.

The second batter made his way into the batter's box, last time up he struck out. Scott and I glanced at each other, and I gave him the sign of a changeup—Klaus looked in, took his windup, and delivered a heck of a pitch. This time the batter was ready for something other than a fastball and ripped it down the third base line, right over Franky’s head.

“Oscar!!” The bench yelled.

Keenan took his position, between left field and second. Arnie was on a sprint over....

“Two...Two...” Roared out the kids.

Arnie was in position to make the play; the ball was hugging the foul line...

“Go two.” Screamed the opposing bench, and the first base coach was waving him on...

This kid was fast, I mean he had a set of wheels on him. Arnie picked up the ball with his bare hand and rifled it into Keenan. The runner was halfway between first and second—Keenan took the ball in chest high, swiveled and threw a dart to Joey. Who was in position. Feet on both sides of the bag—the runner took his slide ....

“Safe!!!!” Bellowed out the ump.... who went into a triple safe indication, to signal that indeed the runner was safe.

“Nice play guys, nice play.” Coach K shared with the team.

“One out, one out.” Again, number one fingers in the air circled around the field.

Scott looked over to the dugout and was given the stop sign to throw down to third if the runner on second was to steal. We were up 3-1...no need to worry about the runner.... Big R moved Kevin, our center fielder, to his left, and told Bruno as well to scoot over to his left.

“Joey...Danny....” Big R told them to take a few steps back, and for Joey to move over towards first a tad.

Klaus glanced over to second, runner in a normal lead and Keenan was giving him the dash over and back move. Klaus looked in, got the sign and threw a curve ball over the plate. It was snapped down...

"Ball." Followed by two consecutive balls in the dirt.... Scott was in defensive mode, keeping everything in front of him. 0-3 was the count. Runner on second got a slightly bigger lead. Klaus balked over to second, then took the stretch.... The pitch, the delivery was on que.... a fastball right down the middle.... Big R believed truly in not walking batters.... make them hit. If we lose, we lose with hits, not walks.

CRACK!!!!!! This kid did it again. He got a hold of it this time.... Deep fly ball to right center.... Kid on second was gone, and nearly walked into score. Kevin was in an all-out sprint.... caught the ball on a one bouncer and hit Keenan standing on second base. Man, I thought, this kid was two for two.... he was a player.... and also, it was now 3-2 us.

"Klaus!!!" Big R hollered out.... clapping, and saying.... "No big deal. Let's get the second out...."

Eyeballing over to first base, Coach K right away noticed the runner and coach were having a rather lengthy conversation.

"Scott!" Coach K made eye contact. Coach K gave him the triple pat on the hip motion.

"One out." The kids again addressed the situation....

Klaus looked in for the pitch, the runner at first had a giving lead.... Scott gave him the 5-down signal, which was the indication of a pitch out—Klaus looked over to first...at his stretch...and picked up his right knee, went past his hips....

"Going, going, going." Our bench yelled out—

With the pitch heading in, and chest high delivery. Scott took a sidestep, got out of his crouch, and took the fastball—Klaus crouched down on the mound. Keenan was moving over to second, he had inched in that way before the pitch. Scott cocked his arm back and threw a bullet to second base—the ump was in position.... again, dust all over the place....

"Out....... Out...." The ump gave a waving fist in the air....

"Two outs." The kids all hollered simultaneously. "Two outs."

"Small ball at its finest." I gawked to my left and there was Ron or Ronny as we called him, chatting it up with me, with a huge grin on his face. "Just like we practiced, Eddie. Just like we practiced."

A déjà vu moment came over me.... It was magical, with no smoke and mirrors, it was like Ronny said, "Small ball."

We never practiced a pitch out except maybe once a month, on a whim or on the fly—it wasn't something we rehearsed over and over, but it was something we never overlooked. Scott had the arm and was athletic enough to pursue that play when the time called for it.... that day, the call came in.

"Danny your way last time." I shot over his way.

Danny gave me the nod. On my notes it said he was a fast runner....and also that he hit the ball off the end of his bat–which indicated to me that he had quick hands. Scott gave Klaus the sign—this time fastball down the middle.

"Foul Ball......." Ump hit both pointer fingers together... "Foul ball...."

Klaus delivered the pitch, "Ball away." Then it went to ball high. Then to full count.

Big R paced the dugout down my way, and said, "On the ropes."

As soon as he said that, the batter hit yet another dribbler, this time to Joey's left on second base.... It took an odd bounce, striking Joey right in the chest, and plopped down in front of him. He took his time. Danny moved over, getting into a split leg position, really stretching out. The kid was flying down first. Joey kept the ball in front, picked it up, gave Danny a one bouncer—and by the skin of his teeth we all heard the umpire call, "OUT...."

It was a photo finish, as if we were at the Kentucky Derby or we would have had to go to New York to make the call. It was so close. But three outs.... Just amazing.

This game was truly turning into an *ESPN* Classic—both teams were fully engaged. Coming off the field, you could hear the rhythm and the rhyme, for the kids were all tethered together. They truly were a pack, high-fives like crazy, pats on the backs, wordsmithing like crazy taking place as they prepared to take on the fourth inning.

Words like excellent, awesome, super, nice, great .... Even though we had given up one run...3-2, it was what was behind the scenes that was the nerve center of a winning team–everyone was together.

“Scott!!! Scott.... Scott....” I could hear a voice piping over the P.A. announcer. It was his dad, Mr. Teafold, right there reassuring his young catcher what a fantastic play it was, and the throw down from behind the plate....

In unison, I heard, “Danny boy.... oh Danny Boy....” I looked up and there was Mr. Reeves giving his appreciation of Danny’s splits on first base....

Danny and Joey were running in, when Big R said, “Nice play guys!!” Which Joey followed up with, “I visualized the success.”—Danny too chimed in, “The vision was in my head.” Once again, Big R’s winning philosophy in full force, he always stressed to the players, visualize your success....

All season the parents gradually got behind the team—one win after another, and multiple losses, too—they bought into Big R’s philosophy. T.E.A.M is all inclusive—we get everything we want, when we all give 100% effort.

Top of the 4th

"Talent may get you on the field, but it's effort and attitude that will keep you there."

~Ken Griffey Jr.

"WOW folks what a game we have going on this afternoon," the announcer went into his spiel. "And don't forget split the pot...we are up to four hundred and forty dollars—so that's two hundred and twenty dollars for you to take home today. Burgers are going fast, and the concession stand will be shutting down at the top of the ninth inning...." The announcer was hilarious—always kept the fans up to date on the food and drink situation.

"Juan, what are we up to?" Coach K sat down and asked.

"Sixty-eight...... Sixty-eight pitches, sir."

Coach K looked over to Big R and patted his left arm—indicating that Klaus was just about at his pitch capacity. Eighty pitches was all Klaus was allotted to make a run at throughout the season. Klaus would start off like Randy Johnson. As the game progressed, he would start to get tired around the sixty-fifth pitch. However, this day, unlike his past, he seemed to be right in there. Still, being in the game, Big R needed to know the count.

There was a quote that Big R passed around to the young men, months ago, it read—

"It's hard to beat a person who never gives up." He would always say, "If The Great Bambino can use this motto, then so can we."

The day he dished that out to the kids, I remember what he said following up that was the key being successful.

"Do your job. If everyone does what they are supposed to, each player will be great, and our team will be amazing."

Big R always had reassuring words. They were demonstrated through his actions. Trust the process. Later that day, after practice, Coach K and I were huddled around the back of his truck—Big R came over. Very early stages of practice, still chilly, jacket had to be worn for this old fart. At least that's how *AARP* sees me, they just sent my first magazine in the mail. Welcome to fifty my wife said.

As we went into our post-practice roundtable, I knew right away that our team was transforming right before my eyes. Coach K matched my thinking and said, "I've never seen a practice like this, I've never seen a level of consistency like this, at this level. These are kids in the eyes of their elders. None can even vote. Yet, what I see on the practice field, is definitely reassuring. We are headed for greatness."

Big R overheard that statement and went into, "Guys what we do in practice, will mirror what we do on the field. Repetition! Repetition! Over and over will bring out the best of each athlete."

"Round n' Round. What comes around, goes around...." Was blaring out of the speakers, throughout the ballpark. Ratt? Once again, I was thinking almost zero fans knew that song, and for sure, none of the players knew that song. But I did...and I loved it.... It was a catchy song, with an excellent beat to it.

In the moment, I was thinking of what comes around, goes around—effort, hustle, continuity, strength, speed, and pure grit. Everything on display today, was basically missing last season. It was all about them, individually. Never a solid bundle of athletes–me, me, me—never WE.... it was a field of individuals on the roster. Our captains last year, just couldn't get a handle on it. Nor could Coach Jones, Coach K, or I...nothing seemed to flow. No strategy whatsoever. Today, it was magical.

"Colton and Phillip, and four more guys come with me," Big R said with a smile on his face. He took them all around the corner of the dugout, outside the fence, and said, "Get warmed up." Which was the go sign for Colton to be ready for the call.

Coach K sat down next to Klaus and went over his innings pitched and who was going to face the next inning.

"Klaus, how do you feel?" Klaus was wrapping his arm up in multiple towels, to keep his it warm.

"Good!" I heard him say.

Coach K went on to express how he had already thrown sixty-eight pitches, a little more than normal.

Big R trusted Klaus. That was clear as day—Earlier in the year Klaus threw fifty-four pitches over three innings and told us he felt great. He got crushed the next inning. We had to scramble to replace him–we did, but he felt awful coming out of the game, having given up two walks, five hits, and four runs scored.

"Coach, I feel good. But I am about at the end of my day."

Coach K replied back, "Okay, you will start the inning, but know Colton is warming up and will be ready to go."

"Yes sir, I understand," giving a thumbs up.

Colton and our back-up catcher, as well as multiple other kids went outside to the bullpen and began tossing the ball. Phillip did not have his gear on, so from afar it looked like six kids tossing, indicating that possibly a pitching change was coming but we could not pinpoint which kid it was going to be. I peered out of the dugout, and I could see Mr. and Mrs. Aries pointing over to the bullpen...they knew their son was warming up. Now for the record, last inning Big R noticed Klaus was a little stiff in a few pitches. He talked it up with Coach K about possibly pulling him—

"Location is good," I overheard Coach K say to Russell–

Big R replied, "I agree. But close."

Scott dug in at the batter's box, this is his second go around.

"He's a hitter...Be ready...." Opposing coaches revealed to the field.

"Strike one! Ball....... Ball......Foul Ball." Ump expressed. He was busy.

The pitcher was rushing his delivery now. You could see he was no longer taking his time. The minute he got the ball back, he was firing it in.

Scott stepped out of the box with a count of 2 and 2, and Big R gave him the swing away. Craaaaaaccccckkkkkk....... a line drive was launched, deep to center field, and I mean deep. Scott made his turn and headed for second with a stand up double. Again, a two baser. Scott was seeing the ball well...and he was now two for two. With two doubles.

"Now batting, number five, Arnold Rivers." Announcement was nearly a whisper throughout the park, after Scott's hit. Cheers, hooting, and hollering were heard all around.

Then it went dead silent when Scott was standing on second. You could hear a pin drop. That smack again took the wind out of the pitcher's sails.

Arnold looked down to third—Big R touched his bill, touched his nose, then touched the bottoms of both elbows. Scott saw the sign and took a bigger lead than normal. Once again, the pitcher took a quick stretch and threw the ball in.... Arnie took the cut, and again, hit it hard to the second baseman.... Scott was not going, but on contact, he took off and was on third. The second baseman made a routine play and threw to first.

“OUT!!” Umpire indicated, with a fist up in the air.

“One out! One out!” All the kids in the field hollered out.

Kevin, on deck, had a very worn-out bat, almost looking matte. It was so faded that the logo of his bat couldn’t even be read any longer. All you could read was a faded, Ma and the I at the end....

“I need a new bat.” Those were Kevin’s words in the middle of the season....

Coach K overheard him say that during practice in the cages. “Why do you think that?”

“You can’t read it any longer—this bat has had it.”

“True,” Coach was sharp-witted and went on. “You were two for four last game with that bat, and you were three for five the game before with that bat.”

“Yes, Coach, but it looks bad....”

“Who said that to you?”

“No one. It just doesn't display well.”

“Who are you trying to impress? Your BA is hovering around .400 and you think the bat looks bad....”

Coach K went on and rounded the kids up at the end of the cages, and asked Max what the length of his bat was–

“Thirty-four Coach.”

“Kevin, grab that bat, and I will chuck some pitches, let’s see how you do...”

Crack, crack, crack, crack—Kevin was ripping them. One after another.

“Well, what do you think?” Coach asked him.

“It sounds fantastic. But it feels awkward......”

“Grab your bat and get in there....”

Coach took his pitching stance, and hurled it in.... crack, crack, crack....

“Enough. How's that feel?” Coach asked....

“It feels terrific and sounds awesome.”

“Of course! It’s your bat.”

“How does it look?’

“Awful. I can’t read it. But it sure can hit.”

"That's the key, Kevin. Looks mean nothing. It's how it feels, and it is what you are used to. Stick with it—after the season is over, get another one......"

Kevin had a learning moment. Flashy doesn't win games. Ability wins games—and that tiny moment was a key asset to the growth of our team—it was noteworthy. It was fun to watch them all look over each other's equipment; they bonded. Even if it was for five minutes.

Kevin approached the batter's box and rotated his bat. Looking over all the scars it had acquired over the season. Kevin looked over to Big R and instantly was given the swing motion—

"Ball high.... Ball down.... Strike one...." Ump shared with the teams....

The pitcher was still rushed.

"Slow down.... Take your time." Opposing coaches were shouting to the pitcher.

Scott had a good lead on third, looking as if he could steal....

"Ball three, outside.... three and one." Ump communicated....

"Come on blue! Where are your glasses?" Fans yelled out.... even a few boos, were shared by the fans. It was a close call, but still a hitters count. Kevin stood out from the box, looked down to Big R—-and Big R hollered out "LET'S GO MARTY!!!.... Let's go...."

Three and one, the coach was aware the pitcher had to deliver one down the pipe.... Kevin gave the nod, and Scott heard the key word.... MARTY was on.... Again, rushed stretch, and short knee lift, Scott was about quarter of the way down now....

"Squeeze play. Squeeze play...." Everyone belted out!

All the fans were on their feet... Kevin squared around and laid down the perfect bunt down first base side—the opposing infielder was playing deep, because last inning Kevin ripped one, so they were not expecting this at all. Scott was flying and slid into home .... The play was to first.... You could see the second baseman sliding over to cover first. The first baseman and pitcher almost collided. Kevin made it down to first on a sketchy half tossed ball—

"Safe!" First Base ump shouted out....

Our dugout was on its feet—Scott came running in, Bruno was right there to give him a high five—

“Nice job Scott.... Great slide....” The kids were going nuts. We were up 4-2....and with only one out, and a runner on first. Bruno looked down to Big R, you could see a hint of happiness in his actions, and it was his turn to deliver.

“Time....” The opposing coach made his way onto the field....

Big R and Bruno met about halfway and chatted it up. In a few minutes the ump made his way out to the mound, and the cluster of athletes broke off to their positions. The coach made his way to the dugout....”

“Take your time....” Opposing coach again told his pitcher. Words of encouragement thrown his way...

“Second or first....” Infielders directed orders.

Scott took a few practice cuts and stepped into the box.

Umpire pointed at the pitcher, indicating game on.

Kevin on first, had a terrible lead, Coach K telling him to keep it simple, for he was picked off in the second....

“Foul ball....” Ump pointed over to left field....

“Ball. Ball two. Foul ball....” Ump shared.

The pitcher was working fast.... He came to the stretch. Big R gave Bruno the swing away sign. The fastball was slower than usual. Bruno was out in front a tad......BAM!!!! Right in Bruno’s wheelhouse, he made contact and drove the ball between short and third—

Our ninth batter was due up—and this was straight out of Big R’s play book. He looked at Max and gave him the double steal call. Max knew what he had to do. The other team looked flat on their feet. First pitch, and Max took his cut. Again, making contact and ripping it foul.

The pitcher seemed so worn out. “Take your time. No Rushing.” The coach from the other team shared with his young gun.

Scott and Kevin made their way back to first and second. Again, Big R gave the double steal sign. Pitcher looked in, and the second baseman made his way in a smidgen closer. First baseman was holding Kevin on. The 0-1 pitch was delivered. Max took his cut and crushed the ball to the second baseman. It was a spectacular play. Short had to make an athletic move to his right and leaped into the air. He made the catch on a line-drive, took about four steps, and tagged second base—

Middle ump was on it. “Out.”

A double play was made right when they needed it the most. Aggressiveness, willingness to take chances, like Big R says, "Sometimes we win them, and sometimes we lose them."

This time we lost them—The fans were going crazy—I even heard a fence kicking adjacent to our dugout— "Man what a play." One dad chimed out....

All the boys on the other team smothered the second baseman. From a coaching standpoint it was a blow, but from a baseball standpoint it was a fabulous play...It would be a TOP 10 for the evening, on our local news Sunday Sports Wrap.

Max made his way into the dugout. "You were robbed......You were robbed!!" His teammates shouted.

It was a poke—but quick feet halted that hit...instincts, too.

Bottom of the 4th

"If you want to be a leader, the first person you need to lead is yourself."

~Mike Sciosia

I looked over at the edge of the dugout—Klaus was unravelling the towels from his arm. Sweats was right there with him, "One pitch, one inning...." I heard him say to Klaus.

A few boys gave him reassurance, "You've got this.... Make it happen..."

The whole bench was in on it now–nothing pressured to say, but out of respect for our ace, his fielders had his back.

I swiveled my scorebook over to the green side, and due up was their number five hitter. Previous at bat he hit a little roller to Danny on first, Klaus covered.

"Danny, your way last time." I yelled over his way–

"Joey—look alive out there." Giving him a heads-up, too. Might be hit in his vicinity.

Scott threw the ball down to second, and a sprightly around the horn commenced. Klaus straddling the mound, looked into Scott, took the sign—1 down and away.

"Ball.... outside." Ump in a dance move, flapping his arms to his right.

"Attack the strike zone..." Big R shouted out....

Klaus looked over—a nod was given. Fastball again.

"Ball.... outside....2 and 0." Ump yelled out.

Location was key for Klaus, not an overbearing pitcher, but a kid you could depend on. I looked over to Coach K, and he gave a tap on his right arm—indicating it was time for Colton to warm up. YES, my lips read.

Big R, still honing in on Klaus, again reassured him.... "Throw it in there. Throw it in there."

"Ball Three." Ump showed the okay sign, and a fist with the other hand.

"Give him something to hit.... don't aim, throw." Big R gave out his repetition of encouragement—

"Ball four.... take your base...." Ump pointed down to first....

Klaus, receiving the ball, struck the inside of his glove numerous times over and over in aggravation.

"Colton and Phil, get warmed up..." Big R pointed at both of them.

"You've got this Klaus!" Could be heard from the fans....

Also blaring out, was, "Man on first, no outs..." The other fans were cheering their team on.

Number six hitter approached the box out of the circle, again looking at the green on the card, "Squared up last time, squared up." I told the kids in the field.... A small lead over at first, nothing major—Danny was holding him tight.

"Go two, or one." The kids were still talking it up.

Klaus took to his hold in the stretch. The delivery was on target, and the young man generated contact. Of course, it was a Texas leaguer—just staying down enough for Arnie to take it on a bounce, the kind of hit, that kids deem lucky. But it still goes down as a hit. Like Coach K says, "A hit is a hit....and a win is a win."

I looked over, and all I could see was Big R's back walking off to the bullpen, getting smaller and smaller.... Klaus still on the hill, man on first and second with no outs.... The ideal situation for the opposing team to rattle off a few runs.

Scott looked over at me, and I held up four fingers—indicating this kid's last at bat was a walk. Coach K was looking down at the bullpen, couldn't see what was taking place...He voiced out, "Scott.... Klaus...." Meaning it was a good time for a speedy team huddle on the mound—he knew Scott would say a few words to Klaus, as well as Franky and Joey—Danny too would chime in.... for strategic purposes, it was to slow the game down. Let Klaus calm down and stop thinking.... Big R always told the kids, "Don't overthink the situation. Great things happen to those who have the will to win." Sure, usually that snazzy slogan worked, but then again sometimes it didn't.

I am an avid reader, love it—and I always give books five stars on *GoodReads* upon completion.... five stars, why is that you ask.... Well, I feel the author took the time to write it. The cover was good. The story may have been okay—but they wrote the book. They published the book. They had the book edited, and that my friends is a huge victory—plus if I learn one thing from that book, then it is five-star worthy—Such as, I would never have written that kind of book, or I would have used different pictures—well, you get the point.

Big R had the same mentality—sure we may lose the game, but we grew as a team. We learned that so and so hitting ninth should be hitting fourth—or this kid has game time speed.... We learn on every loss.... We never focus on the bad. We learn from it. Change it up. Refocus the drill—or simply, we as coaches must explain fundamentals more clearly. Get dirty with the team and show them first-hand how it works—be better than we were yesterday.

First and second—still no outs...The opposing team was now really into it.... screaming, yelling and flat-out going nuts over there.

That reminds me of the day, Big R shut our team down.... We were up six to nothing against a rival school, one where all our kids knew the other team's kids—and our team stepped out of their zone and entered the *Twilight Zone*. Kids were throwing out unacceptable comments, which were then heard in the stands by our fans and parents....

By the time I heard a very offensive outburst—Big R called out to the umpire...

"TIME BLUE...."

Instantly the umpire gave him the podium. Big R stepped out of the dugout, approached the backstop fence, and addressed the fans. "We don't do this. We don't accept this....and no parent or fan will act like this."

He shut it down. Then he made his way into the dugout....

"Sit down and shut up!!!" Dr. Jekyll turned into Mr. Hyde....

"Boys, who wants to be on this team????" They all raised their hands, as pale and white as a sheet of paper.

"Then act like a team—this is baseball. Not a backyard fight—we show respect and right now you are disrespecting our school, our team, and our community. Show respect for your parents, the other team, and all the umpires.... KNOCK IT OFF!!!!! NOW!!!!!"

I had never seen a coach pivot and become a manager in such a short amount of time. He was Coach Russell—but in that brief five minutes he had to become the manager. Managers must lead and handle situations when they are called for....

Respect for Big R grew a million-fold on that day. One, the kids never saw that side of him before. Two, it was called for.... and he did it with authority, with bravery, and with dignity.

In the trenches, anything and everything goes. We all were in the arena that day. We lost that game, and deservedly so. We lost our cool, but Big

R created a lesson for us all. He doesn't approve of childish behavior on the field or in the stands, he reassured the team of that. At the next practice Big R shared phone call after phone call that he had with parents, including the Athletic Director, and the principal of the school. They all thanked him and appreciated his leadership.

The seventh batter took his stance. Klaus peered over to second, Keenan was not close to the bag. Again, Klaus took a swivel over and balked it—a fake throw over...

"Batter, Batter.... focus on the batter." Coach K blurted out....

Klaus was getting tired. Beads of sweat were pouring from his forehead, and he even had a salt stain gathering around the perimeter of his hat. The sun was now full blown, and not a cloud could be seen in the sky—perfect day for baseball. The baseball gods were enjoying this game, and I am sure they were all looking down, talking strategy and what ifs....

Klaus focused on the batter— "Strike one...." Blue called out....

The opposing team was ranting and raving. They had toned it down a bit, but were still getting waffle irons, because their faces were imbedded in that galvanized steel.... Fun to see them all on their feet—I know, appreciation for the game always gets me, love it.

Sitting next to me was Little Timmy, chewing his gum so frantically, like he was gnawing on a piece of corn.... As I looked down the bench, all the kids were gnawing on something or taking a swig of something. All eyes were focused on the field—still no outs....

"Ball high......" Blue shared—he shared a bunny and a fist in the air—

"Ball two...." then, "Ball three...."

Big R made his way back to the dugout. He gave Coach K and me the thumbs up that indeed Colton was a go....

Klaus got the sign. Fastball. He delivered, and crack, the batter drilled it to left field.... Arnie lined up his path, and on an all-out sprint he made a diving catch.... he popped right up and threw a dart to Franky on third....

"Time...Time...." Was called by our third baseman.... Umpires all held up two hands and time was granted.

"One out guys! One out!!!" Infielders held up #1 sign.

"Hey Blue…." Big R called out and started his stroll out to the mound….

Klaus knew right away that was it…. All the fans were on their feet, our team was outside the dugout, and greeted Klaus with a few high fives, pats on the back. Even Little Timmy, sitting next to me, a kid that maybe played four times in a season, gave him a hug—kinda funny to see, an underclassman giving an upperclassman a side hug…. Klaus took it all in, with a gigantic smile….

With a little break in the action, all the infielders gathered up on the mound. Big R had one rule for relief pitchers, and you could hear it a mile away— "Nothing fancy…. throw strikes…. trust the guys behind you to make plays."

Colton took control of the mound, and Big R made his way back in—

"Five!" Ump yelled out…. "Five!".

Colton took his freebies, gained his composure on the mound…and just like that….

"STRIKE ONE…. STRIKE TWO…." Ump called out….

Still man on first and second…. one out…. "Keenan be ready! Franky look alive!" I blurted out…. signaling the ball was hit their way last time. CRACK…. Batter made terrific contact with the ball, again hitting it over towards the gap between third and short. Franky made a dive to his left and the runners were going. The ball was hit hard enough to find the seam. Arnie was too deep in left, trying to keep everything in front of him—Third Base coach was waving in the runner. Colton darted home to back up Scott and Keenan was in position for OSCAR.

"Left… Left…. Perfect." Scott called out to Keenan….

"OSCAR!"

Arnie heard the words and threw a stinger to Keenan's chest……

Scott called, "Two, Two…."

No play at the plate, run scored. As rehearsed, Keenan took the throw, turned to his right and hurled the ball over to Joey. Joey now had the runner in a pickle. He was right in the middle. Runner on second was on third…. a showdown took place, rotating each player from Danny to Joey. Bruno slid over to first and on a throw from Keenan applied the tag to the runner….

"Out.... OUT...." First base umpire yelled.

Bruno looked over at third and rifled the ball to Franky....

"Back.... Back...." Third base coach called out.... headfirst slide back in.... Franky applied the tag....

"Safe.... Safe...." Ump called out, and he was in the perfect position to make the call......

"Time.... Time...." Franky called out and walked the ball over to Colton....

"Two outs.... two outs...." Kids yelled out....

Colton took to the mound—with a runner on third base.... Coach K came over and sat down next to me—Big R had a funny grin on his face and gave us both a thumbs up....

As Coach sat down, Klaus came over and said, "Shakespeare couldn't have planned out that last play any better." We looked at each other, Klaus continued, "You don't know.... Shakespeare is the one that created that phrase. 'How camest thou in this pickle?' it was in his book, *The Tempest*." As Sweats handed him a grape Gatorade out of the cooler.

"To be or not to be... that is the question...." Then he marched off.... Coach K and I looked at him, then at each other and just had a hearty laugh....

"There he is Coach—there he is.... the switch hitter.... I told you so. You owe me one bag of pickle sunflower seeds...." Ronny exclaimed to me.... and sat right there with me.... Low and behold he was right—bottom of the second he was batting left-handed and now in the bottom of the fourth he was batting right-handed.

"Look at his cuts. Stronger this time than last time. Seems to be more natural...."

"Ronny, you are right.... good eye kid.... good eye...."

A strike out was his last at bat, when Klaus was bringing the heat—Colton was a high 70s and very low 80s pitcher—and based on the cuts.... I hollered out .... "Look alive...."

Again, seeing Vs in the dirt—kids were ready.... The runner on third was jumping around like a jackrabbit, trying to distract Colton ....

"Batter.... Batter...." Franky threw his way.

"Strike one...." Ump said, and that cut of the batter was ten times better on the right side than the left.... Ronny was right....

Colton peered in.... glanced over to third—Franky pointed at the batter. He took his hold and rifled the ball in, and contact was made.... Ball was hit right up the middle...and it was hit hard too.... Runner on third scored and it was back to zero to zero–all tied up 4 to 4....

Instantly, I heard, "You've got this, Colton—you've got this..." It was Klaus on his feet, blazing hot and wearing his jacket, with a huge bulge on his left elbow—you could see the wrinkles of the towel protruding through.... He was there cheering his replacement on, and he was there cheering his teammate on...

"Kevin your way last time..." I hollered out...

Kevin held up his glove.... Sure, enough like clockwork—One more pitch led to our third out—a towering high fly ball was hit about ten feet to Kevin's right ....

"I got it... I got it...." Webbing of the glove was open, the ball hit dead center and his other hand collapsed down on it.... two hands proving worthy again.... it never fails.... two hands worked. The inning was over....

Klaus executed his job, went eighty-one pitches before being taken out—Colton same thing, get in, hammer down, and get outs.... Yes, runs were scored, but to watch the kids move around on the field was awesome.... Do your job! Know your job! Well, that coaching philosophy just worked.... We were in this game as a team... All engines were a go, and the kids were having fun....

"Hey Logan.... Logan...." I heard my name called out, and I stood up and peeked around....There was my wife at the edge of the cinder block wall—

"Need anything?"

"Sure, a bag of peanuts and Diet Coke would be great..." She is always there—and always at the beginning of the fifth inning she comes down and checks on me. She too, was 100% invested in this season. She knew the last few years I questioned why I still continued to coach.... fun was never in a sentence. This year it was.

Top of the 5th

"No matter what you have achieved or accomplished, keep pushing to get better. Don't let good enough be good enough."

~Kris Bryant

As the kids all came off the field, each one of them greeted Klaus and told him how great of a game he pitched. Not a single one wandered off to focus on himself. As a unit, they all shook his hand, and gave him complimentary words of praise—just awe-inspiring to witness.

Big R was right there and looked over at me and gave me a wink. Coach K was clapping his hands like crazy.... We were all welded together. As *The A-Team* put it, “I love it when a plan comes together.” Big R’s plan, which was now all of our plan, was thriving.

I can recall one of the first practices, way back in early March—Big R and Coach K were talking it up. Kids one by one were mustering up, practice was about to start. All the kids gathered around the edge of the dugout. Sweat’s doing his thing, and I was just walking over to all the players–

“Good afternoon, Coach Eddie...” Nathan threw my way...

“Hello Nathan...good day to be outside, isn't it?”

“Yes sir.”

Then one after another; “hello,” “let's play two,” “let's go guys,” “hi Coach,” “hello Eddie,” followed up one after another. The previous seasons, most kids just kept their heads down, and shut their mouths. Intimidation was an understatement. Not too much chatter. There was no vision for the team to see.

Big R looked over his shoulder at the young men, he, and Coach K in stride, asked all the kids to have a seat.

“Men, we have a vision—not only for the team, but for each and every one of you. Some will get a ton of playing time, others will be limited, and still others will be in and out of the games as need be.”

Big R’s hands were always in motion, as if he were giving a motivational speech. He couldn’t stand still—could have been a traffic cop in downtown Tokyo. I am sure he could whisk the traffic through, keep the pedestrians moving and just enjoy the non-stop action.

“Vision.... What I see over the horizon will take each and every one of your individual talents to create a winning team. Moreover, it will create unity among all of you. When the time is right, and you are called, you will be ready. But it’s what we do in practice that will generate Ws and will forge a winning team. Wins and losses do not define a team. What defines a team, as you will see, is the willingness to give effort, both mentally and physically."

Coach K spoke next, "Everyone on your team is important.... Importance knows no rank...."

Instantly all the kids looked at Coach K, with huge yeses and a smile....

"No, no, no.... thattttt.... wasn't me.... that was Mike Krzyzewski. The head coach of Duke.... I just simply gave him a few words to say one day...."

With that, he laughed, and all the men chimed right into the humor. The team was all in. WE could feel it, we could hear it, and we could see it.... When young men, actually engage with a coach, it's a vibe that can't be taken away. The vision was creating tentacles and pulling us in, tighter and tighter with each practice under our belt.

"What we do today, will take us across the finish line, and we will do it as a team." Big R always had words of encouragement—and that very sequence is how we started off the top of the fifth inning.

I swiveled my scorebook over to the red side. We were up to bat. Coach K and Big R were dashing off to their spots.... Keenan had already made his way out to the on-deck circle—dousing his bat with spray pine tar, concentrating on his swing—good, clean, crisp cuts...nothing out of control. It was a disciplined swing, elbow back, nice explosive stride, with eyes seeing the ball in. He was one for two thus far, a bunt and a dribble of a hit back to the pitcher.

As the other team took a few ground balls, and back over to first—I could hear a second pop, a sound that someone is warming up. I looked up and, sure enough, there was another pitcher down by the bullpen, getting in his tossing.... Nothing major, but a simple toss...The starting pitcher made a few less than threatening pops, nothing like he had done in the first four innings—he looked worn out.... The other coach, too, was making preparations to have an exchange. If need be...

The windup and the pitch. Keenan gave one heck of a swing...

"Strike ooonnnee!" Ump called out....

"Way out in front. Sit on it...." Big R said, then gave him the swing away motion....

“Ball......outside....” Which was followed up by “Ball in.” Then “Strike two...” Ump was on it—kinda close. Could have gone either way. But he was consistent all game...nothing out of character...the ump was a veteran, and in a game like this, consistency is key.

“Two and Two.” Ump spouted out....

Keenan dug in his back left foot a little deeper and was at the ready. A less than stellar heater was on its way. Catcher had his mitt a little low, close to the dirt, trying to get Keenan to swing at a bad pitch.

CRACK......

Keenan drove the ball to left center, right over the shortstops head.... running full speed, and making a small turn at first–eyeing Coach K and holding up for a single—

“Time blue...time....” Big R shouted—”

With that, Bret stood out from the dugout with his helmet already on. Prior to Keenan’s at bat, Coach K suggested that if Keenan gets on, let's put wheels at first for a pinch runner—Big R agreed.... Bret and Keenan exchanged a slap on the way out and in—Bret took his lead off at first....

As Keenan made his way in, high fives and “atta boy” greeted him—the whole dugout was on their feet—

“Nice job Keenan.... Fine job son....” I could hear the fans and even his dad holler out.

“Now that's a way to start off an inning....” I looked down, and with a thumbs up, Greg, our backup shortstop, was cheering on his teammate....

Last year, just three hundred and sixty-five days ago, almost no kid would cheer on another kid if he was the backup—jealousy, pure jealousy. Today, and all season, it was “I have your back....” “I support you” and “we are in this....”

“You don’t have to have a title, to be a leader...” Big R stressed that to us all— Back-up or starter, we were all in this together.

After Greg spoke out, the bench chatter started up...momentum was flourishing. I sat there, took a sip of my Diet Coke, and cracked open a few peanuts....

“Peanuts, get your peanuts here....” I looked over again, and this time, Arnie, Klaus, and Sammy were doing their best vendor impersonation, while I was cracking a few.

Hilarious. I loved those days, prior to covid, when vendors would walk the aisles of the ballpark—rifle a bag of peanuts over, and pass across money–

“Keep the change,” I always said. Unless it was a $20—but I always took plenty of $5’s and $10’s to the game–

My wife and I loved venturing up to Cincinnati to catch the Reds, and even drove over to Louisville to catch the Bats. I may not have been a ball player, but I love baseball—for baseball has been very very good to me....

“Now batting, number fifty-five, Danny Reeves...” P.A. announcer shouted over.

I didn’t even hear Keenan get called before–that was how much I was into the game....

Danny was 0 for 2. Both hits were hard. One to third and one to second—so Danny was due. Bret took his lead. It was always three and half steps off first for Bret—normally just three for the other kids. But Bret was quick reacting and as fast as Shohei Ohtani. Danny took his stance, and the pitcher took to his stretch...

“Back...” Coach K said....

“Safe....” Ump called.... Nice move over for this late in the game.... Bret took his lead again, and again...

“Back...” Coach K was on it.

“Safe...” Ump called—-

“Batter. Batter. Batter....” Opposing coach screamed out.... meaning forget the runner, go for the hitter....

Bret glared down at Big R—the steal was on.... Danny in his right-handed stance got the call—Pitcher to the stretch, knee went past his waist.

“Going! Going! Going....” Other team yelled out....

Bret was off to the races, with little specks of dust flying off the back of his cleats. He was barreling down, head down, and as fast as a lightning strike, he began his slide. Catcher had a great arm, but the ball was thrown down and inside to Danny. Throw down to second was off to the left of the shortstop covering.... he was pulled off the bag...

"Saaaafe..." Ump bawled out....

"Car wash.... Car wash...." Our dugout called out.

Everyone smiled in unison. Big R looked down at Bret. Coach was bent over, right hand and left hand on his kneecaps. Bret nodded.... Danny saw the call, gave Coach the nod.... Pitcher took to his hold, looked over to Bret...he had a great lead, bigger than normal.... He looked into the catcher, made his delivery....

"Going, Going, Going...." As quick as Rickey Henderson steals took place, another steal was underway....

Our bench was up at the fence, hands grabbing the inner linings, and bills of hats thrashing the chain-link ever so hard....

This time the catcher received a perfect strike, cocked his arm, the typical catcher's throw almost like Joe Burrow throwing a football, and hurled it down to third. Third baseman was in position, ready to receive the throw. The toss was on its way.... Umpire in position to make the call.... Bret, with his wheels, had a terrific first step, and exploded right out of the gate. It was going to be close. Dust kicked up; the player took the swipe......

"Safe!" Umpire screamed out.... and went into about five more motions to indicate safe....

"Oh, come on Blue—did you leave your glasses in the car?" I heard a fan shout out...then that was simply smothered by roaring cheers from our fans and his teammates...

The count on Danny was 1 and 1—runner on third....

POP...POP.... POP.... I heard the sound of leather popping. I peered down at the bullpen of the other team. A pitcher was now into his ritual—catcher had full gear on and was warming up the pitcher. I knew something was cooking. I had a smell for it.

"Danny, drive it.... drive it......" I heard the kids say.

Danny peeked over and gave a smile, knowing his teammates had his back.... Unlike anything I had ever seen, game after game, these young men were behind each other. I was right there, alongside of them on this journey....

Pitcher looked over to Bret. Nothing major. Simple lead and standing in foul territory. The pitch on its way, Danny sat back and waited. Crackkkkkkkk.... Danny got his first hit of the game, a nice solid connection and drove the ball up the middle... one bouncer before second and rolled into center field.... Bret scored easily....5 to 4 us.... and still no outs.

"Time blue.... Time...." Opposing coach walked out of the dugout—pointed down to his bullpen.

With that, the pitcher was out. Excellent game that kid pitched, however, the innings were grueling, scorcher in the full sun, and at the fifth inning, it just seemed right to take him out...

All the fans, both sides, gave the kid a standing ovation. Everyone knew he gave his all, and Coach K and Big R were clapping right along with them—it's a sign of respect that Big R hammered into us. The kids, too, were ever so faintly clapping.... our team clapping for someone else, not before this season—there would have been little extracurricular activity last year and years before—smart aleck remarks...like, "About time..." "See you later alligator...." "It's over......" Not today, not one peep of disrespect was heard out of our players.... Big R had cut that conduit off months ago.

Danny and Coach K talked it up at first.... Pop, pop–the young man on the mound had some heat....

"Okay Joey you've got this...." I heard the kids say...

"Look for bunt.... scoot in...." Opposing coach, giving instructions to the kids....

Joey was 1 for 1—slapped up the middle and a walk.... The other coach was now starting to grasp that small ball was in our toolbox, and we weren't afraid to use it.

Big R glanced down to home plate and gave Joey the swing away motion. Joey wasn't a power hitter by any means, but he always made contact. Danny took a simple lead off the bag; pitcher came to the stretch. Not once looking over, he was focused on the batter.

"Strike one...." Ump shared.

Joey took a massive swing; he was way late.... kid on the mound had some umph....

"Strike two...." Blue shouted out—held up his fist and bunny ears......

"Protect the plate...." Coach K threw his way....

"Contact...contact...." I heard Big R say. Joey choked up on the bat. Pitcher again had zero interest in Danny at first. He had a speedy set up and delivery. Danny was not given the green light at all. Protecting his base at all costs....

"Strike three......" Blue went into his left arm out and pulled his right arm back motion.

Joey chased after what I thought was a changeup.... back-to-back fastballs, then he laid off the gas and caught Joey way out in front.... Great pitch sequence I thought....

"One down...." The opposing team all shouted, and held up the number one signal......

"Now batting, number forty-four...." Franky was 0 for 2 today thus far.... Franky was a hitter, he loved fastballs. As he took his approach to the batter's box, he heard,

"Hit it! Hit it!" Big R shouted.... meaning fastball will be first pitch—-unload on it...crush it....

Danny took a few steps off first.... Pitcher now threw over...

"Safe..." Ump called—wasn't even close, just a soft lob over....

Franky dug in his back right foot, a couple half cuts at the plate. Pitcher took his delivery and as Coach called it, the fastball was hurling in. Now for the record, Franky had walloped a few dingers....and crackkkkkk his bat made contact, thrusting the ball in a trajectory like a surface-to-air-missile launch. He got a hold of that one and drilled it to left center. The ball exploded off this bat, like a sound that could be heard around the world—Danny was in full throttle, Big R was giving him the wave. Franky was ninety feet behind him....

"Third! Third.... cut-off man. Hit the cut-off man...." Other team was yelling tactics.

Our dugout was on their feet, as Big R waved Danny on.... rounding third and heading for home.... Franky was in a dead out sprint, making a terrific turn at second base....

"Third, third...." Kids hollered out......

Cut-off man, the shortstop was in position to receive the ball. He looked it into his glove. Franky was twenty feet away, hustling to third and on a terrific throw, the cut-off man drilled the third baseman a ball about six inches off the dirt, right in front of the bag...just as Danny slid into home for another run........ Franky slid in and this time, it was an easy call....

"OUT!!!!" Ump shared with us all....

"Six to four us...... Six runs......" I heard Sweats call out....

Franky hustled into the dugout, and the kids welcomed him in with open arms.... Fist bumps all around.... What should have been a double, turned into an RBI, and a sacrifice out.... Big R knew there was a ton of commotion going on.... Franky wasn't very fast, and with only one out and us up by one, pushed the game to its limits...a visionary was coaching third....

"Now batting, number seventeen...." The PA announcer called out. Scott was two for two—batting .1000 for the day. Two outs and no one on base. This time the pitcher could take his normal wind up. Scott had already socked two doubles.... Scott was a righty, Big R and he exchanged signs—hit away was given.

Pitcher took to his windup—and it was a fastball, waist high, but about a foot inside.... Scott had to jump off the plate a few, no harm no foul.

"Ball.... inside..." Blue threw his hands to his left....

Scott composed himself, and dug in—good half cuts. Pitcher took to the windup. Again, a fastball, about chest high, and way inside.... Scott had to turn his back to the pitcher and whammmooooo.... Scott was pegged by a fastball in his back, right below his left shoulder.

Scott fell down to the ground. All the fans were on their feet. Our team and their team were at the fences looking in. Like a pogo stick, Scott popped up.... Umpire pointed down to first.... Scott stood up and exchanged the evil eye with the opposing pitcher.... It was a Mike Piazza and Roger Clemens moment—a spaghetti-western movie was underway, as if a high noon shootout was about to take place. Scott walked four steps towards first. Big R and Coach K were almost to home plate. Opposing coaches were out of the dugout and the umpires were closer than normal. Scott took four steps which turned into a slight jog. Then, last twenty feet, a dead out sprint to first.... Scott was moving his shoulders around.

"You, okay?" Big R shouted...

"Yes sir! I am good."

Coach K was right there and talked it over. Scott held his pain back. He winced. You could tell it stung—but he was a tough kid.

A few months back, into our third game of the season, Scott had just blasted his first goner. In his next at bat, he was beaned by the opposing pitcher—only this time, Scott charged the pitcher. Instantly it turned into a Nolan Ryan and Robin Ventura boxing match—this time Robin won the fight. Scott took off for the mound, pitcher was running away...Scott grabbed him and got one good swing in, making contact with the kid's left shoulder—chaos ensued.

"NO! NO! NO!...." Big R yelled out.

Big R, the opposing coaches, and all the players were on the field. Like a ringside coach, Big R grabbed Scott, gave him a huge bear hug, picked him up and whisked him over to our dugout....

"Sit down...calm down...." He told Scott.

As I was standing on the field that day, everything came to a stop as quickly as it started. Big R took charge, and the opposing coach wrangled up his team. All quiet on the western front....

The umpire walked over to the opposing team, pointed at the pitcher, and pointed off into the distance. He then approached our dugout, pointed at Scott, and gave the same gesture—both players were ejected from the game....

We ended up losing that game by one run. A game we should have won. We lost our composure. We lost our will to win, and we let our tempers fly. Later, after the game, all us coaches had a meeting. We all knew what had to happen. Scott was suspended from the team for one week. Meaning two games.... Scott's parents Mr. and Mrs. Teafold were right there with us. They both understood the significance of the fight. However, one thing I do know is Big R explained to us and to Scott's parents, "The flame in him is strong—don't let it burn out. He is a leader. He is a super kid, and we love having him on the team.... but my rules are my rules....no fighting...."

It was hard not to see Scott for seven days. The players missed him. The young ones looked up to him. Catchers are the leaders on the field– "Next Man Up!!!" Coach Russell always had an answer for everything. With that, Phillip got the start behind the plate for a few games, and he did great.... That first practice back after the incident, an impressive speech was given by Big R—

"No one is bigger than the team. Scott is not gone. He is just on a seven-day sabbatical. Let this be a lesson, men. One small outburst can cost us a game. Just like we lost—it's a distraction to all of us."

Coach was right—things happen. But he had to address the situation instantly, quickly and as a manager, he did.... Even though as a coach he wanted Scott behind the plate—his skills radiated for the whole season. Parents respected him. Players respected him and even Scott respected him.... Respect is not given, it is earned.... Big R earned it.

This game, Scott exchanged that respect back, by hustling down to first—he had learned his lesson. Sure, he was in pain, but not as painful as sitting out seven days and missing two games a few months back.

"Now batting number five...." P.A. announcer in a crackling voice, blared out.... you could just hear a slight pause, like I am sure glad nothing bad happened. Scott on first, with two outs....

"Batter! Batter! Focus on the batter.... Two outs.... Two outs...." Kids giving their pitcher reassurance.... we have your back.

Our dugout was still on their feet. Little Timmy made his way over to me and sat down next to me.

"Great job to Scott.... Man, that has to hurt.... Getting clobbered with a fastball...."

I looked over to him, "Peanut?"

"Sure, thanks." He said and cracked one open. Throwing his shells under his feet and crushing them with his cleats.... Kids will be kids. It never changes.

We sat there and mulled over the situation together—I took a few sips of my Diet Coke. Kinda warm now, ice was all gone and kinda flat.... but I had to wet my whistle. Timmy, took a swig of orange Gatorade...

I looked over and Sweats was cleaning out the dugout—PLASTICS were now filled, nice and neat—kids all began to take their seats....

Big R looked in at Arnie. “Swing away Big A.... Swing away....”

“Strike one....” Blue called......

Arnie stepped out, looked down.... swing away was given......

“Strike two....” Ump called.... “0 and 2,” he shared with the pitcher....

First pitch Arnie looked at, second was a half-speed swing....

Deep clapping in our dugout, could be heard.

“Come one Arnie,” players hollered out. “See the ball, hit the ball...” I heard a fan say....

Arnie dug in his left foot—

“Foul ball!” Ump called....

“Good rip, Big A. Good rip...” I heard Mrs. Rivers call out....

From my standpoint, Arnie did not look comfortable at all. Having seen Scott get pelted with a fastball. I think his brain was in protective mode. Pitcher took his stretch and hurled a fastball. Arnie didn’t even try to swing.... Psychologically Arnie was had.

“Strike Thhhreeeeee!!” Blue went into his K motion....

Backwards K... I thought as I put the pen to paper—backwards K. Unlike Arnie.... But we were up 6 to 4.

Bottom of the 5th

"I don't know any other way to lead, but by example."

~Don Shula

Big R came over to me as we were about to take the field. "Watch his motion.... look for the knees being bent...." as he looked at Colton taking the mound.

Colton was good for about two to three innings, but this was far from a normal game.... This was the kid's biggest game of the year—We never spoke about the next game, till we were ready to face the next game.

Coach K always said, "Loose lips, sink ships..."

Meaning chatter about something that hasn't taken place is just gossip or rumor. He always told the kids, "Today is a present. It is a gift for what tomorrow will bring...so use today's gift to our advantage."

As the sun was getting a little deeper in the West, this game was far from normal. We hadn't seen this kind of talent all season, and we were the team that would take on other top teams...to test our skills. Today, it was a dream of a game. All wheels were turning, the game was intense, yet fun. It was heart pounding, yet joyous—

Colton was about to face batters he had never seen before. And through four innings, watching from the dugout, he knew the coliseum atmosphere of Rome was in his wake.

He was a gladiator of an athlete—two-star athlete too. Starting QB on the football team, yes, he was used to warrior games, being in the foxholes with his teammates. But as Big R stated early in the season—OUR BEST IS THE BEST.... Colton had an impressive year as a starter. 8 and 3—should have been 9 and 2. I still think that call for the third out was a safe slide—Oh well, no reason to create should haves in my brain—but he should have been safe....

What's behind us is gone, today we are present.

"Two...Two...." Scott called out. Hurled the ball down, and like a team, they whipped the ball around with a ton of zip and high-level energy....

"Strikes.... Strikes...." Coach K shared with Colton.... Indicating he knew the pitch....

"Look alive, Franky.... Your way last time Arnie.... Both kids gave the nod to me.

Colton waved his glove our way, Franky took a few steps back, and Arnie motioned in and took a few paces back. Scott put down the one sign. The number two hitter had just ripped a double his previous at-bat, and ripped it with authority....

Players were chatting it up, “You've got this 45, you've got this 45....”

Colton's nickname was Colt 45—not the old Houston MLB ball club, but a shooter—we were in an Alamo showdown. Colton counted his paces.

Colton took his wind up, and threw a heater just off the plate, inside...

“Strike One...” Ump shared.... Scott pointed right at Colton—

“Nice, Nice....” Kids in the dugout were sharing.

I walked down to Big R and shared with him that the next batter due up was two for two—single to right field and triple in his first at bat....

“Strikes, strikes, bend the knee...” Normal chatter from the stands.

Colton looked in, Scott gave him the two sign and swiped the outside of his thigh.... Got the call. Windup and the pitch, WIIIIFFFFFEEEEEEEED

“Strike two...” Blue called out—

“One more 45. One more kid...” Calls were coming in....

Scott looked over at Big R and saw him touch the top of his head. Scott knew the call...Immediately, he squatted down, gave the number 1, and touched the top of his mask. Colton’s delivery was precise, about shoulder height, and the batter took his swing...

“Foul Ball.” Blue shared and threw up a fist and bunny ears.

“Okay, kid. Okay.” Kids hurling 45’s way—

Scott threw down the number 1 again, and again touched the top of his mask. The delivery was right on target, this time the batter and the fans could hear Blue shout out.

“Strike THREEEEEEEE.” Blue went off to his side and did his K dance.

Scott cocked the ball back, catcher's throw off to Franky to third, Franky to Joey, Joey to Keenan and Keenan to Danny—Danny back to the mound. He walked it in, handed the ball to Colton and yelled, “One OUT!!!!”

Colton got the ball—looked in at the batter. This kid was a player, 2 for 2—but we never shared that with Colton–

“Strikes.... Strikes....” With that Coach K stepped into the dugout, after waving all the outfielders to drift back almost to the warning track– “Keep it in front.... Keep it in front....”

Scott gave the sign, one down. Batter had that look to him. Nothing fancy. Just a gritty player—No sleeves. No shin guards. Nothing hanging out of his back pocket. No jewelry and wearing two missed matched batting gloves—you know, worn out, too.... Nothing brought attention to this kid, other than his bat and his athletic ability.

"Come on FOUR.... FIVE." The fans blared out ....

Colton looked in. Took his wind up and hurled in an amazing fastball.

BOOOOOMMMMMMM!!!!!!

"You got all of that.... get out of here.... get out of here." Fans were yelling.

This kid jacked it so far, left field, and fish-hooked two feet to the left of the pole....

"Foul ball." Ump shared—this was not a foul ball by any means. This was a no-doubter, that just curved.... like hitting a one wood on a narrow fairway, just barely off the bent grass, a little from the high grass.... Just missed it—The sound was beautiful to hear. But, scary for our team to witness—like anything in life, the will to win was deep today.... both teams wanted it. Blue threw Colton a game time ball, the shiny, new ones were long gone. This one came with dirt, spit, grass, and had a few marks on it. I always liked those. The grip was better.

"0 and 1," Blue shared.

Scott threw down another 1 and dragged his right hand on the dirt—signaling keep it down, down below the knees, maybe even shin high.... Let's give him nothing to hit again. Colton took his windup, and threw a heater down, and I mean down, it grazed the home plate.... Scott scooped it up....

"Ball down..." Ump pointed to his shoes... "One and One." Blue shared—

Colton received the ball and took a little crescent loop around the mound—he bent down, picked up the rosin bag, gave himself a few bumps on the top and bottom of his hand. Batter took a few practice swings—Fans were throwing out a few words—Colton got the sign, number two away—the pitch was delivered, and this time it was another BOOOOOMMMMM......Deep to left center, and I mean deeeeeeppppppp......Arnie was on his wheels to center, and Kevin was on his horse to left......Going. Going. Going. Gone.... A four baser was just handed to our team. It was a YAK like no other—perfect connection, perfect swing, perfect Yakety Yak.... The batter never tossed his bat, nor did he fling his arms, or rub it in to Colton, as other hitters did. He hustled around the bases. I even heard Franky exchange a few words. “Nice poke.” Respect was given and respect was earned....6 to 5 us....

“One out—one out...” Our team held up the number one fingers....

I looked down at the scorebook, #4 hitter was due up. Today he was one for two, a little tap to left field and a dribbler to Joey at second.... Colton took the ball, looked in, and rifled it....

“Ball high....” Blue shared—

Momentum is something I do believe in, but our bench was still reassuring #45 with clapping and talking it up. Ball one hastily took to ball three.... followed by a strike and a wiff, then blue called out, “Ball four...take your base.” Big R looked at me, and smiled, but knew Colton was frustrated with the gopher—

“Colton! Trust them all...” Big R shouted out—

The #5 hitter in the circle walked up to the batter’s box. Today he was 0 for 1. Hit to Danny and a walk—

“Danny your way—Joey be ready...” I called out.... Coach K moved Joey and Danny into position.

Big R yelled, “Strikes! Strikes! Strikes!!!!”

Colton came to the stretch, glanced over his left shoulder, just a small look and threw the ball in—CRACKKKKKKK......Fastball was drilled between short and third on a line drive, one bounce on the grass and rolled into left field. Arnie was on it, he had seen a ton of action today....and threw the ball to Keenan on the edge of the infield—

“Time...” Keenan called...walked the ball up to Colton, looked him in the eye. “You’ve got this four.... five.... you've got it....”

#6 hitter was due up—two for two thus far today. Bunt and hit to left field, I shared with Coach K—

“Arnie.... Kevin....” Coach K, with an invisible bullhorn to mouth, hollered out, and gave the signal to back up, back up.... “Your way...”

Colton took to his stretch, the kid on second appeared to be slow—not a lead at all. As a matter of fact, it was about one step or two at most.

Colton looked in—Fastball was zipping in, crackkkkkk again. This time not as forceful. The kid got underneath it.... lazy, high fly to right center....

"I've got it, I got it," Bruno called out.... Runner was at the ready, and the ball was deep enough for a tag up—

"Going! Going! Going! Third.... Third.... Third...." Kids called out–

Like the majestic throw of Bo Jackson to home plate, Bruno caught this ball in stride, took a hop, and on a one throw, launched the ball on a two bouncer to Franky on third. There was Colton right behind him, to take the backup. Joey on second was lined up—the throw was on target—dust bowl was created, and the swipe was on the money...

"Out!" Third Base Ump called out...." The kids were going crazy.... Complete frenzy. Like they had just won the lottery....

Complete mayhem ensued. It was riveting to watch the play unfold. Fans, right outside the dugout, were cheering their tails off. In the distance, over by the opposing bench, I even heard, "What an arm.... What a throw..."

Those words rang true because of Big R's willingness to consistently run it at practice. Let's take it from the top.... Like a director overseeing a Broadway play in the early stages. Big R knew repetition would take hold. It did, and we all witnessed it.

The kids all ran in, smothering Bruno on a terrific throw and running side by side with Colton. He, too, was greeted with open arms in the dugout.

A double play to end the inning. Now that was a great entry in the scorebook.

Top of the 6th

"Coaches who can outline plays on a blackboard are a dime a dozen. The ones who win get inside their players and motivate."

~Vince Lombardi

"Folks get your grub on.... nice cold slushies, piping hot, hot-dogs and burgers.... Concessions stands are still open. Oh, and 50/50 split-the-pot is now up to four hundred and twenty-four dollars—you do the math. Nice night out after an amazing game." P.A. announcer belted out—then he went right into *JUMP* by Van Halen.... Might as well JUMP.... JUMP.... I looked over at the kid's dropping gloves on the bench, picking up helmets, grabbing bats—talking it up.... overhearing enthusiastic words thrown around. As soon as JUMP was sung, I saw half the bench all jump—

That song must have been forty plus years old, yet it's still heard throughout ballparks, arenas, stadiums, and on commercials. Kids knew it, sang it and I even gave a little air guitar solo.... The Bench was psyched....

Big R and Coach K went over to the red side of the scorebook. Out. Hit. Hit, and a deep flyball.... Those were the markings of the batters due up, last at bats.

"Now batting, number twenty-eight, Kevin Snow." The announcer rattled off.

Kevin was two for two today.... punch into left field and a bunt....

"Let's go Kev.... come on Kev.... Let's go TWO EIGHT" Kids on the bench called his way.

Bruno proceeded up to the edge of the dugout, and there was his dad, Mr. Vogel—

"Nice play son...nice play... See the ball. Hit the ball."

"Thanks.... Okay, Dad."

Bruno took three steps up, entered the on-deck circle, picked up the weighted donut and slid it down the handle to the fat end of the bat—he began to warm up—I even saw him touch his toes and hold it for five seconds—Stretch Armstrong impression.... very limber, then again, all the kids were. Coach K and Big R stressed the importance of stretching. "No pulled muscles, hold it for five." Constantly heard throughout practice and pregame....

The pitcher threw his last warm up—a quick around the horn.... Kevin took his position outside the batter's box.... Big R gave him the swing away motion.... First and third baseman were creeping in, maybe they were guessing a bunt. Windup and the pitch....

"Strike one." Blue handed out.

Kevin, a left-handed slugger, was within striking distance of hitting .300 leading into the game. Last season, Kevin got very little playing time—he did play, but was not a starter. Not too many sixteen-year-olds make the starting lineup–

In the off season, Kevin worked on his attitude, his maturity and grew tenfold as a young man. The key to a great teammate is dropping the ego, and realizing there are other kids as good, or better than you.... Athletic ability was never Kevin's problem, it was his boo hoo attitude. All about me.... never focused on the mission of the team.

The first day, back in February, Mr. Snow following a few indoor practices, approached Coach K and had an amazing one on one conversation—Coach K shared with Big R and me that he and Kevin worked on his.... TEAM.... MATE.... attitude.

Last year, Kevin had the look. He had the feel of the game, but when things didn't go his way, he basically shut down... barely could even speak to me or Coach Jones.... We gave him every chance to share his thoughts. He would pull his head in, a turtle reaction and duck and tuck into his core shell—We both did everything, everything, but we just couldn't get Kevin to understand bad things happen to good people–

It wasn't until the end of the year party.... Some parents and I were celebrating the season, when Kevin approached Coach K and thanked him for a great season....unlike him, but on the last day he became a team member. He stepped out of his comfort zone, took on his inner beast and shook his hand. I wish I knew what he said... K just told me later on, Kev indeed would be back, with a new attitude and a new outlook on what being on a team consisted of.

At the beginning of the season, Kevin was our backup center fielder, an older kid named Alex was our starter—great kid, eighteen-years-old, veteran by the baseball Dictionary... Unfortunately, prior to the first game, Alex was running in his neighborhood, and got his ankle caught in uneven asphalt, maybe a pothole. He fractured his ankle....and was placed in a boot—a boot he would have to wear for five weeks, conduct rehab, and if things went his way, could possibly play again at full speed in ten to fourteen weeks.... Nearly the whole season was gone for him....

In the early stages of practice, Big R never focused on one kid. Nor did Coach K—it was all about the team.... If it was a drill for all, then everyone did it. We were not inundated with talent all around. Maybe one or two kids would even be considered for Div. I baseball. One kid, maybe, for an MLB draft—

Big R told them all, "It's the US that will win the games.... not you, not you." As he pointed to them all individually.... "I promise you this." He would hammer in.... "I promise you we all will get playing time.... but we all have to be ready, at any given moment to play. What we do over the next twenty days, will decide the next four months—give it your all. Work hard, here and at home... Be ready."

Kevin stepped out of the batter's box—Big R again, gave him the swing away—the confidence he had in Kev. Pitcher took his windup and delivered a slow, hanging curve ball. It was enough to throw Kevin off balance. It was inside, too...He swung, tangled up his feet and slammed to the ground....

"Strike two." The Ump shared and looked down to the ground. "You okay, son?"

"Yes sir...I am good."

He popped right up from lying down in the batter's box.... He looked right into the dugout—a look of what did I just do????

"Nice Houdini." Alex yelled out—yes Alex, the very kid with the boot on...sitting right there and said, "Kevin you've got this... You got it...."

Kevin regained his composure, looked down to third—

"Drive it...drive it." Big R, smiling and clapping, said with gusto.

He adjusted his batting gloves, pulled his helmet down and adjusted it.... Took a few half cuts, dug in his left foot...

The pitch was on its way—could have been the reaction of the swing, but a fastball was called—BING.... Kevin drove the ball right over the second baseman's head.... and Alex and his teammates were at the fence...

"Way to go, two.... eight...... Way to go kid." Alex looked over at me and I gave him the finger point.... What no one else knows, besides us coaches and teammates, is Alex stayed on the team.... He worked one on one with Kevin—they both batted left-handed. Alex the senior, the master, the black belt, took Kevin under his wings and schooled the young apprentice. Giving him the confidence and maturity Kevin so deeply needed—

Alex was the line leader. When other kids would have washed out to sea, Alex stayed on and basically became a baseball consultant–something I am sure a few business moms and dads in the stands could appreciate from a teenager.

"Play at two..." Players in the field, yelled out....

"Now batting, number seven." The announcer called out.

Bruno was one for two—single and a strikeout—Bruno looked down to Big R—Kevin too, looked over. Coach gave the swing away sign, as well as took his hat off and brushed his hair over, numerous times, over and over.... Kevin knew the call—

Big R called out, "Swing away, Bruno! Swing away...."

The call was nothing—Big R always liked to keep the opposing team guessing, steal or what. Pitcher took the stretch, looked over to Kevin, with a three-step lead—knee went past his waist and Kev gave off a clever twist to his right.

"Going.... Going.... Going...." Everyone belted out.

On que, it was another pitch out.... This time, Kevin was not going. Just giving the impression of stealing. Big R got the other team thinking.... Kev and Bruno looked over again–swing away. This time, he had both hands on his knees—hit and run was on.

Pitcher took a glance—delivered a hurling fastball. Bruno took his swing, and drove a line drive right over the shortstops head–Kevin bolted down to second...

"No outs—third, second or home." Kids called out.

"Now batting, number ninety-nine, the designated hitter, Max Carlo." P.A. announcer called out.

Max was one for two—hit into double play last at bat, and singled to left field first at bat—Max looked down to Big R—nothing was said, just a simple double clap....

"Don't leave them out there on the pond..." I heard the fans state....

“Drive them in Max! Drive it.” I looked to my left, sure enough Phillip and other players were expressing enthusiasm to their teammate.

Max stepped in. Pitcher looked over to second—from the stretch released the ball.

“Strike one.” Ump called out—

Max took a good, crisp cut, missed it by a hair. Pitcher again threw the same pitch—this time, Max got underneath it.... It was a towering ball, nearly straight up in the air—the hang time was impressive.

“I got it.” Shouted out the catcher, as he spun himself around. Two or three steps in front of home plate....

“I got it!!!!!!!!” This was really yelled out...Pitcher over called the play. He had the natural instincts and was coming in. He could see the whole play shake out—catcher moved out of the way. With his glove up, the pitcher made the catch.

“Out.” Blue shared...

“One out...one out....” Other team held up #1 finger—

“Nice play pitch...nice play.” I peered over to the bleachers, and sure enough it was Mr. Carlo who shared those words.... Good on him I thought...

Max exchanged a low five with Keenan.... Keenan was two for three today. Single and a bunt.... we were up by only one run—getting late in the game.... only three more innings to go—Big R stared down. Keenan, a left-handed batter—gave him the sign to drive the ball—Left-handed batters are harder to steal third on. So I knew with their catcher's arm, no way was Big R going to call a steal.... I was right.

“Drive it, Keenan. Drive it....” Big R clapped and stated.

Keenan dug in, took a few licks, settled in and on the first pitch, drove the ball hard to the second baseman—pulling to his left, and with no other direction to be made...he threw the ball over to first...

“Out.” Blue shared—

“Way to move them over Keenan, way to go kid.” Keenan gave a smile as he ran into the dugout—kids right there with a few fist bumps, forearm hits....

“Play is at first....” Other coach shared his guidance....

Danny was due up next with two outs and runners on second and third. Kevin was fast.... took his lead at third. Danny dug in.

"Ball outside." Umpire again with his arms in motion. Man, this guy was good....

Danny looked down again to Big R—like holding an axe, Big R chopped away and clapped over and over. Danny took a huge cut, whiffed.

"Strike one." Blue pointed to his right....1 and 1 up in the air, giving the signals to all to see.

Danny again got multiple claps, and the drive sign by Big R.

"Ball inside..." Blue again waving inside...

Deep, hearty claps were now given by Big R—giving an indication to keep his back elbow up; he was dropping it too quick. Pitcher looked over, sweat pouring down his face, his chest was drenched with sweat—gave Kevin the once over and delivered an amazing change up. Danny was way behind, thinking fastball, he flinched forward a niche, regained his composure and created a half swing, to protect the plate—

"Strike three." Blue called out.

The kids all rounded up their gear—words exchanged, like "We will get them next inning...protect this house." Under Armour would have loved that one—but it was a catch phrase the kids all grew up with.

I looked over. Sweats was jogging in back from the on-deck circle—like stage crew behind the scenes that never get the spotlight. Sweats was working his tasks with pure passion. He organized the helmets, picked up the pine tar, the weighted bat and doughnuts. His organization was impeccable...such a sight to see. The only reason I looked over, was because Little Timmy was right there with him, placing all the equipment in the correct spot—Last year it was all Sweats. This year all the kids were Sweat's right hand men.....even Kevin, the kid with the attitude problem and Alex with a boot on earlier this year, were carrying equipment....It was art in pure form....Unit of one......amazing to witness.

"What are we up to?" Big R inquired.

I was fast with my reply, "Twenty-seven pitches so far."

Colton was a little ahead of his pitch count. Big R pulled Coach K over and said, "When we get through this inning, we need to go to Allen.... that will be enough for Mr. C out there. Keep the arms fresh and let's win this."

"Deal."

Coach K walked over to Phillip, tapped him on the bill of the hat, "Let's warm up...."

Six kids left the dugout and proceeded down to the bullpen to toss. Allen was right there with them...he knew his time was coming. The call was right around the corner.

"Head in the game," I always say. "Look alive too," always chime in with that notion...As we all settled in the dugout, kids took the field.

"Squirrel...." Hank blurred out.

Squirrel!!" Quick coach, give me one of your peanuts.

I handed him one—SSSHHHH Hank held his finger over his lips, in other words, silence.... Hank tossed the peanut on the field. Squirrel ran up to it, picked it up and took off.

"We will not see him again."

The young outdoorsman just gave us all a lesson, and we all just laughed it up. A memory that I know I will never forget—out of the clear blue, in the middle of the big game, a player turns into a wildlife conservationist, and it worked....

Bottom of the 6th

"A good coach will make players see what they can be rather than what they are."

~Ara Parseghian

The squirrel was gone—headed for the Sweetgum trees I would say.... game on.

The best of the best, were within one run of each other—one run. As close as close can be. Between innings I sat down with Colton and went over the first three batters and what they had done in previous at bats—a few good rips. Including hits, walks, and fielder's choice.

Colton took the ball from the base of the mound, looked around the outfield, revved up his engines, and took his warmup pitches.

“One batter, one inning at a time.” Coach K shared with the team, with his fake bullhorn to his mouth. Coach K’s scratchy voice was more prevalent now, deep and howling.

“Get one—get one.” Big R pointed out to Colton–he glanced in.... gave the nod. A swift around the horn took place. Umpire pointed at the pitcher. Fans were totally in on this game, for this was the big one...Each game is the big one, but this truly was the big one. We needed this win to lock in our Championship game. This Super Regional final set up the North vs the South in a showdown next weekend—but that was seven days away.

“Today is our moment...” Big R shared with our team before the game as we huddled up. “We never focus on the next game at all,” as he hammered in, “It's today!!!!”

Big R chimed in, “Colton—focus on delivering strikes. Trust our players.”

“Yes coach, I will.” Colton shared solemnly answered. He knew the significance of the game. It was discipline that got us this far—nothing out of the ordinary, no heroics, and no Superman.

Colton got the sign from Scott—last at bat this player manufactured a nice pop to left field....

“Arnie,” Coach K got his attention—again, clapping. “Your way last time. Franky look alive, you, too, Keenan.” Players acknowledged the cue.

“Foul Ball.” Blue called out....

“Nice pitch.... kid.” Player shared his way.... two was put down.

“Ball outside.” Blue swept to his right.

Scott squatted down, threw down the two again. This time—Craaaaccckkkk, nice connection was initiated. A two bouncer, hit extremely hard, up the middle—Kevin came running in from center, just outside the infield dirt, scooped up the ball, quickly hurled it to Keenan on second...

"No outs, play's at second!!!" Kids all yelled—

Due up next was the third baseman, having a good game on the field, and was one for two—

"Arnie—again..." Arnie gave a tip of his cap, signaling he was ready—Big R to Franky— "Over two, over two."

Colton glanced over to first, no big lead—Danny straddling the bag. Colton looked in, got the sign. A curveball—nice too. BANG!!!

"Foul Ball!" Ump shouted out—ball took a wicked line drive off the end of the bat and into the bottom of the backstop, between the dugout and home. Kids, on the other team, went crashing back into the dugout. A few parents and young children close to the screen were scared half to death. That's why they have the warning sign posted.

Keep All Hands And Fingers Off The Fence

That reminds me of a funny story. About the tenth game of the year, the opposing team was up to bat and hit a towering foul ball. Very few spectators were in attendance, and it was an away game. The ball was on a vertical trajectory, nearly breaking through the atmosphere, then it began its descent. Scott threw his helmet off, spun around, looking, looking for the ball. Our whole team was up, pointing straight up into the sky.... Scott's feet were jumping all around, like he was stepping on hot coals—

Bruno was pitching, and he was standing nearly on home plate. The ball hit the top of the cross bar, then took a two bounce on top of the dugout, rolled around five feet, then fell off. Lo and behold the ball landed on Jeff Cash's grandpa's lap—as he was sitting in his camping lounge chair....

It was straight out of a *Three Stooges* bit—Big R standing right there, saw the commotion firsthand—

“You okay sir?” I heard him say, and he flew out of the dugout, locking both hands and fingers in the chain-link, having a one-on-one conversation with Jeff’s grandpappy.

“I am fine, I am fine.”

Jeff’s dad was right there too, “He's good coach. A little startled. But he is good.”

“Dang, spilled my pop....” I heard grandpa say....

“Sweats! Sweats!”

Big R reached into his back pocket and handed Sweats a $20—“Sneak over there, find out what he is drinking and buy him a replacement on me.” Sweats took off.... A few more at bats took place, Big R still 100% invested in the game, kept peering over to Jeff’s grandpa—This time, making eye contact—Grandpa held up his pop, gave coach a wave, huge smile. Sweats made his way in.

“Thank goodness they had orange drinks at the stands....”

He began laughing, and I was laughing too—Big R overheard it and laughed—then the whole team went into a laugh.

A simple gesture of kindness, an instant reaction—Not rehearsed. Not practiced. An act of genuine leadership took place.... One simple act of kindness, from a manager of a baseball team—most folks would never have checked on the man. Moreover, none would have bought him a replacement—Big R did....

Jeff made his way over, came back and looked up at Coach, “Thank you sir, thank you Coach Russell—My grandpa can’t make it to too many games. Dad taxi’s him around cuz he can’t drive any more. You made his day that much more special.”

Big R looked right at him, “We are all in this together little buddy–all of us.” The two fist bumped.... “One more thing Jeff, give your grandpa a game ball–and you sign it. Give him a memory from our team.” “Great idea. Thanks coach.” Special moment topped off.

Colton got the sign—Scott put down another curve, hitting the outside of the thigh, with his glove down over his left knee so the opposing coach on third, couldn't see the sign. Colton took to the stretch, peered over to Danny...pretty good lead—he kicked his left leg back,

“Going! Going! Going!” Infielders and bench hollered out....

It was a slow curve, the kid sat back and waited, this time driving the ball to Joey's left, and within reach of Danny's right. Danny just tall enough, made an amazing play. Took the fast roller, with momentum to second, Keenan had moved over to second base, on a rifle. Danny struck Keenan in the chest about two feet from the bag. Joey was now curling around, taking over first base. Keenan, took the chest high throw, stepped on second.

"Out!!" Umpire called.

With momentum now shifting towards first, Keenan chucked the ball over to first. Joey with his right foot back, extending out, scooped the ball up on a one bouncer....

"OUT!" First Base Ump called—

"Double play!!!! Double play!!" Bench and fans were screaming at the top of their lungs.

Our bench went nuts—I mean nuts. Like fireworks on the Fourth of July—explosive in a matter of seconds.... Every kid and every fan was on it. "Nice play. Way to work it. Great vision. Nice Joey.... Nice Danny...."

"Discipline guys.... Discipline...." I heard Franky yell out...

It's one thing to take ground balls indoors, since it's only half speed—limited space, limited roof, kids flying around everywhere—

Big R on our second official practice hammered in two words- "Small ball and discipline." Yes, that was straight out of the horse's mouth.

Coach K and I knew discipline, having played Division I baseball, and being around sports for years—we understood it. But small ball and discipline, those two words were hitting home with us both, and were in the early stages with the kids.

"Run it again, run again," with space limited, we could only set up a first and second base—and the kids took the drill in, one after another. Big R and Coach K were right there explaining the technique, explaining getting in position, reacting to a play. Fungo bat in hand, Coach K would hit soft balls to first baseman then it would go, 1 to 6 to 4—

"Do it again! Again, first to short, to second standing on first."—Big R exclaimed. He liked what he saw, then shouted, "Again! A tad quicker!"

Boom, before long, we moved from indoors to the field—and as we had rehearsed, we went to live speed....1 to 6 to 4—fungo bat now was live.

Coach would hit them between first and second—Joey would swing around, sometimes he could make the play. Sometimes it was within reach of Danny. Keenan would cover second, Joey would cover first.

Discipline got us the double play. It looked hard from an outsider's perspective, and believe me, some of the kids made it hard. Big R included everyone. It was an all-hands-on-deck play. Something we routinely practiced at least two times a week, and it never stopped there. He would shift to the same sequence for Franky at third, Keenan covering third, and Joey sliding around to cover second—plus all the pitchers knew what to do, back them up on third, and Scott would run down the baseline to cover behind first— "Action!" Big R and Coach K always said. "No motion—Action."

"Who is due up for us next inning?" Big R said to me.

"Joey, Franky, Scott and Arnie—Arnie is 0 for 3..."

"Okay, if we get on base—I want to make a change with Arnie. Replace him with Jason.... Jason got a few good hits when we put him in, so he is due...."

"Sounds good..."

"Jason, get loose..." I tossed his way...

"Yes sir, Coach."

"Two outs. Two outs...." Kids all held up bunny ears—

"Up the middle last time....Keenan. Joey be ready" Coach K with this fake bullhorn singled out.

Colton had two outs, bottom of the sixth—

"One more! One more!" The fans behind me were really cheering. "Strikes. Strikes. Strikes..."

Colton locked in the call, batter up was one for two. Nice hit and strike out....

"It's him again, the switch hitter." I heard the call. This time the young man was batting right-handed again, just like last time. "Scott..." He looked over and I gave him the one sign....

Colton took his wind up, and on cue, fastball high—wiffffffff.

"Strike one." Blue called.

"Again!" Called out Big R—

"Strike two......" Blue called. The batter chased it again with a gale force wind following his swing ....

"Again...." Big R called....and sure enough—

"Strike three......." Blue threw out his left hand and pulled back his right...

"That's three outs." Sweats said, as he hustled by me to the cooler—with two green Gatorade squeeze bottles. It was hot. Without any signal, without being told, without being directed. Sweats ran out to the first base umpire and offered him a swig. Dashed over to second, same thing. Crossed over to third and finished up at home plate. He took his steps down into the dugout. "Let's go guys! Let's go!" I looked at him and gave him a thumbs up.

Big R made his way in, Coach K and I sat down—

"How many is that?" Big R asked

"Forty-four pitches." Juan instantly called out.

"Okay—we are near the end. Let's get Hawk ready for this inning..."

Hawk was really Hank, our third starting pitcher. He was a gifted left-handed pitcher, the youngest of all our pitchers, just sixteen-years-old. But this kid was tall, six foot two, and had a nice rocket booster for an arm. He had been a little wild at times under pressure in the past.

Big R and Coach K worked with him, day in and day out. Each outing, we all allowed him to gain confidence. And mid-season, he went from a 6.32 era to a 3.75 in just a matter of five outings. Discipline took him the extra mile—believing in himself and believing in this team. He was not a finesse pitcher at all in early March. He truly thought he could overpower the batters. Some games, he couldn't even last one inning. With some growing pains, he grew tenfold and settled down.

Coach K took him under his wings, as well as Colton and Klaus. The two senior players explained all season, that doesn't have to be fastball after fastball—curve, change location, all the amenities of a great pitcher—not just 80 miles an hour, like batting practice was needed....

"Phillip, Hawk, over to warm-up some. Take Allen, Sammy, Jeff and Johnny with you—short, under control toss down at the bullpen please..." Big R gave the motion.

As Coach K stood next to me, he shared, "Always at the ready."

Yes. Big R was always thinking two steps ahead.

He bolted down to first. Big R took his spot at the little mound of sunflower seeds, just outside the coach's box.

Top of the 7th

"If my uniform doesn't get dirty. I haven't done anything in the baseball game."

~Rickey Henderson

We were up 6 to 5, great game—fast game too, for a few innings, and a few innings were over the top. Typical baseball game: highs and lows—you work through them. Joey was taking his swings on-deck. The opposing pitcher was hitting the glove, not as much pop as before—but good tone to it. Joey was one for two with a solid hit, a walk, and a K.... Nice fielding today though, he was a player–always listening, growing, and making himself better.

Back.... n.... Black faded off to, “Now batting, number sixteen, Joey Breen.”

“Let's go kid—drive it.... get a hold of one....” Fans and our bench cheered.

Big R gave him the swing away call—Joey stepped up to the batter's box. Franky was in the on-deck circle—

“Get one.” Opposing team hollered out .... “Get one!”

“Bend! Bend! Bend!” Opposing coach shouted out–with that, I knew the kid, at least in the coach's eye, was beginning to stiffen up. Maybe reaching the end of his mound presence.... I took a mental note.

Joey dug in. He had quick hands, good eye for the ball—making contact was never an issue for this young man. He stood in, looked again down to third—hit away motion was again given. He dug in, pitch on the way.

“Ball high.” Ump called–

I now understood the bend call. Pitcher looked dog-tired. Joey glanced down, Big R gave himself a simulated poke in his eyes–again,

“Ball high....” Ump called.

Now I was seeing it, and the last signal in, Coach Russell saw it too.... Again, glancing down, Big R gave the two-hand fist, or hold sign.... Meaning take another....

“Ball high....” Blue declared again, with a fist and three fingers up in the air—swiveling around for the fans... “Three and O.” He called out.

“Drive it.” Big R shared down ninety feet to Joey—he took a few cuts. Adjusted his batting gloves just a bit tighter, dug in his back foot—pitch was coming in, Joey waited back, took his cut. Again, the ball nearly shattered into pieces.... Drove it right up the middle.

Hustling down, Coach K was there to welcome him, as he took his turn to second, and walked back to first—

"Nice jack, Big J...." I could hear his dad, Mr. Breen, blast out. Fans were cheering.... Coach K already had the sign, he was going...

"Now batting, number forty-four." P.A. announcer doing his best Vin Scully rendition, shared with the fans.

Franky was one for three. Double, walk and a hit to right. "Eddie.... Eddie.... Get Jason ready...." The call was on. We would pinch hit for Arnie now, due up fourth, and make the change out in left as well. A veteran player would be replaced by a junior player.

Walking over, I tapped on Jason's hat. "Get ready, get ready.... you're batting after Scott..."

"Yes, sir.... Yes, sir...."

Jason exploded off the bench, gathered all his gear. I walked over to Arnie– "Arnie you are going to sit this one out...Jason is going to bat and take left field."

"I understand...." He said, and not a peep was exchanged again. He went into rooting and clapping for his team, as if it was no big deal. Let's win this game.

Next man up philosophy was written on the walls—Big R earlier, in the second pre-season game, explained to the kids that at any given moment an exchange of one player for another could be given–-"I don't care if you're a senior, a junior, a sophomore, or a freshman, when the time comes, you will be replaced for the greater good of the team."

His philosophy would create a ton of chatter among parents and the players. Out of the twenty-five players making the squad, half the parents understood the significance of "team." Some had never seen their kids get removed from a game, and others, well, they had never seen their kids enter a game while the game was going on.

"We are here to win, and we will win with all of us doing our part— Pinch runner. Five pitchers in one game. Sitting one out. Replaced due to hitting or fielding."

He shared it with them... "This also entails, we root for each other. We don't pout. We don't talk bad about each other, and we don't question why we are entering or leaving the game at the moment. I will always explain why."

Big R was amazing at explaining his reason. Last year Coach Jones would never elaborate the reason. He would just say, "You're out, and you're in." The vagueness created a ton of animosity on and off the field—Coach Jones spent a ton of time after hours on the phone with parents, and that heartache then would be reflected on the field. He could never shed the monkey on his shoulder's—he never could decompress. He carried the weight of a manager, not conducting himself as a coach.

Franky got the cal—the call from Big R for the hit and run—Joey got the sign too from Coach K—Pitcher took to his stretch...

"Back...Back...." K threw out.

Pitcher made a great throw over, just missing the right fingertips of the headfirst slide back.

"Safe!" Umpire yelled out. The international call with his hands, over and over. Man, these Umps were on it....

Peering down—Franky made eye contact with Big R—a quick double clap, with a "Drive it." Joey now had a three-and half-foot lead down at first. Pitcher took to his stretch, paused, looked over to first, then rifled it...

"Going. Going! Going!" Kids on the other team were yelling out....

Franky got a hold of it and drove it to left center......right over the shortstop's head, amazing connection, bat to ball. Joey slid in, of course there was no play—

"Play at third, second or third...." Kids on the field shouted out.

"Time blue.... Time...." Opposing coach called.

I looked over, and Coach K gave us the double tap on his right hand. Two kids popped out of the dugout and dashed over to their bullpen—warm-ups commenced. At any given moment, a new pitcher would enter the game—Scott was due up next, and he was standing with Big R on the third baseline, halfway talking it up.

"Joey, Joey." Coach K said, and reinforced, "No outs. No outs..." Coach pointed at his head–our team loved that indicator. The sign for BE SMART and use your noggin.

"On the pond Scott.... on the pond......don't leave them out there." Kids on our bench shelled out....

Kids were moving like crazy—Jason was doing some sprints just outside the fence—getting stoked to get some playing time. Helmet was on, batting gloves were on...." Opposing coach cleared out the huddle around the mound and made his way back into the dugout.

"No outs.... get one.... get one...." Kids again, giving each other the play is almost everywhere....

"Now batting # 17." P.A. announcer chimed.

Scott is two for two, and of course was hit by a pitch...

"He's a hitter, he's a hitter." Fans threw out the reassuring words.

Scott looked down, Big R instantly gave the swing away, acting like he was driving the ball, with his head down and a quick hands sign. Pitcher peered over to second, glanced over to first, and hurled the ball in. Scott took a massive cut, very unlike him...

"Foul ball." Blue called out....

"Scott, no hero.... Contact...." Big R followed up with, "Stay calm! No fences. Let the bat do the work." He again gave him the swing away.

Scott dug in, took a fastball down and out....

"Ball outside..." Blue shared—

Jason was on deck, getting his rips with the motion of the pitcher. Again, another pitch, fastball down and away.

"Ball two." Ump shared holding up 2 and 1....

Scott dug in, getting the swing away sign.... Ball making its way home was instantly elevated, sky high within the vicinity of the second baseman...

"Infield fly.... Infield fly.... Infield fly." Second Base Ump yelled out—

"One out.... One out...." Kids held up #1's all over the place....

"Let's go Jaaassssoooon... drive them in." Jason was a sophomore, a great multi-tool player. He could hit, field and could play just about any position if asked...with the exception of catcher. That was not in his forte. Jason is an amazing young man. JK is what the kids called him, for his last name was Knochelmann.... Plus, all the kids grew up with *Harry Potter*.

The craziest part was, just two weeks into preseason, Mr. Knochelmann was about to pull Jason off the team—which, would have been a shocker to the program.

Jason was good, but not great. Jason was gifted, but not developed. Jason had a great baseball mindset, but could not grasp the TEAM MATE concept.

One morning after a terrific gym practice, way back when, Big R rounded up Coach K and me, and with a clear explanation, he told us that the Knochelmann family was indeed onboard with the program.

The night before, after practice, Mr. Knochelmann had approached Big R and explained that his son was deserving of playing time and should be a started—he was on a travel ball team.

Travel ball is a very touchy subject when dealing with players and parents at the high school level. Today, it is easy to say you're playing on a travel league—pay some money, play on weekends only, and boom you are part of a travel team.

Big R that evening explained in grave detail that there are tiers in travel ball—Elite, Gold, Silver, and Continental (beginner). Through honesty, empathy and respect for Jason and his parents, Big R had to explain the whole concept of travel ball. Through Big R's guidance, he explained that it was in Jason's best interest to not quit the team, hunker down, work hard, and grow as a player—not just pay to play. Mr. Knochelmann understood the situation, thanked Big R for explaining that not every travel ball player is equal—he compared it to Big Leagues vs Single A. Yes, they are all good players, but the great keep advancing up. The upper tier is for the elite, the lower tier is for kids to be a part of something. With room still to advance up, as they mature.

I am sure Mr. Knochelmann did not want to hear the truth, but true honesty must be front and center in any coach—Big R was that example. Once again, he faced it straight on—and who knows what will happen, Jason could very well make the elite squad. The whole season, Jason was developing, owning the concept of we are all in this together.

I am so glad he was there, and not Mr. Jones—Mr. Jones would have just said, "That's the way it is." Not Big R, his kid-glove approach always won over parents, our school, and our community.

"JK.... JK.... get your pitch..."

"Strike one...." Ump called—-right down the pipe, little lower than waist high, but in his wheelhouse—

You could tell he wanted to take one, to witness the pitcher live. He stepped out. Big R gave him the swing away.... Next pitch was high. Followed up by a great cut—but missed...... one and two...

"Protect the plate!" Kids called out. JK choked up–

"Joey be ready...be ready." Coach K threw his way.

Crackkkkkk.... Jason, with the barrel of the bat make excellent contact, he got underneath it, drove it to right field, faded right, hugged the foul line—Right fielder had a great angle to make the catch.

"Go go go." Big R shouted to Joey—with the momentum going forward. Big R knew the kid would have to make a great throw—Joey tagged up and took third with a stand-up steal.

"Two outs... Two outs.... Play is at second or first...." Infielders shared with one another

Jason ran into the dugout, instantly you could hear, "You did your job.... You advanced the runner.... Nice JK.... Nice job..." Fans and his teammates gave him a round of applause....

Kevin was on-deck. Runners on first and third......Big R gave Kev the sign, hit away. We were still up 6-5 and Big R is a firm believer in that you need to be aggressive on the bases.... The steal sign was on for Franky. Pitcher took his stretch.... Franky, bigger than normal, and Joey had a nice lead at third.... Pitcher got the sign, in his delivery...

"Going, going, going," Catcher received the ball a tad high.

Franky was off, I couldn't believe it, but the catcher actually made a throw towards second base—only this time, it was designed play—as the throw was off, "Go," was told by Big R. Joey was headed for home—The second baseman was not even close to the bag—it was a direct throw to the second baseman, who caught it and threw a bullet back to the catcher—Joey took his slide. Another dust bowl was created—car wash moment in motion....

"OUT.... OUT...... OUT...." Home Plate Umpire called....

What a play at the plate for the third out. Through my eyes Joey was safe, but Ump was in great position to make the call. Clearly, he saw it differently....

"Great hustle Joe Joe." Kids told him, and it was... Perfect call, at the perfect time—it was 100% offensive. Big R always stressed more is more—don't take a step back when ahead. Be in the game and see it through at all costs. Big R had a way about him, willing to make educated transactions for the benefit of the team. Momentum, we have to keep it on our side.... On that play, momentum clearly shifted to their side...

I know if Big R would do it again, he would do the same thing. Keep the other team on their heels. This time they caught us on our toes—

"Great play...." Big R shared with me as he approached me in the dugout.... "Is Hawk ready"—"

"Yes, he is..." I replied to Russell...."

"Colton!" Big R walked with him out of the dugout– "Get one. Get one..."

"Yes, sir."

It's funny to hear the kids say "yes." Early practice in the gym, all Coach K kept hearing was yeah...... yeah... yeah this.... yeah that. K told me and Big R how tired he was of hearing yeah. "Wish the kids could say yes...."

Immediately, Big R said, "Hit it." I blew the whistle—he rounded up the kids— "Mock interview time, Danny right here.... he said."

"Danny, do you like baseball?"

"Yeah, Coach—"

"Done. Sammy, do you like hockey?"

"Yeah, Coach."

"Done. Franky.... Do you like third base?"

"Yeah...."

"Done. Sweats, do you like this team?"

"Yes, I do...."

"You are hired—" Big R shouted out and shook Sweats hand. "Welcome aboard slugger." He then motioned over to the team, "Okay guys, which do you think sounds better, yeah or yes????" Big R panned around, looking at all the kids. Immediately all the kids said, "Yes!"

“Then yes, it is....no more yeah.... If you like the way that sounded, then so do I!!”—

“Hit it, Eddie.” I blew the whistle—

“Back at it...” Big R said... The group broke off, back to their drills.

“Coach K,” Big R said, then followed up with, “Your words are always welcomed on our team.” Big R shook Coach K’s hand—and hustled down to a drill.

“Well, there you have it. He has our backs.” Coach K winked at me, gave a laugh, and said, “I love it.” Last year Coach Jones never took a coach's suggestion. It was always under consideration—not today, we were in this together.

“Folks, we have a monster of a game going on.” P.A. announcer called out...and into his monologue. “Concessions are still flowing. Split the pot is growing, and if you want to hear a tune, come on over and I will make it happen.” Slight pause....

Then with a Harry Caray voice, he launched, “Everyone on their feet. It’s the seventh inning stretch... On a one! On a two! On a one, two, three, four...”

With that, the philharmonic conductor led all the fans in, *Take Me Out to the Ball Game*.... I heard it, looked over and sure enough, up and down the fences I could see dads, moms, grandparents, and the bleachers all singing to the famous baseball, intermission, stretch tune.... It was awesome to see, hear and take in.

Bottom of the 7th

"Success isn't something that just happens–success is learned, success is practiced and then it is shared."

~Sparky Anderson

"Coach, do you like Iron Maiden?" Mike Stillwater, sitting next to me, asked.

"Why do you ask?"

"Eddie, Eddie—that is their figure that represents them, and today, we are making the other team run for the hills..."

I laughed so hard. Here we are nearly thirty-two years apart, and Mike knows all about Iron Maiden...

"Wonder if they would play one of their songs???" He looked at me, a huge smile came over his face....

"I doubt it."

"Well, they are playing AC/DC and Van Halen... chances might be good." He laughed and I laughed—Mike and I shared a little rock-n-roll moment between innings...

I said, "Let's just stick with peanuts and crackerjacks."

"Root. Root, root for the visiting team." He threw back to me quickly. Realizing we were the away team....

Funny things kids say to coaches, but it strikes a chord—communication from management to employees—Big R encourages us to talk about anything with the kids. "Talk it up." He would say, "Anything is better than silence." Getting kids to talk baseball, school, work, family, weather, it didn't matter—just volley a conversation back and forth....it was amazing. Last year, kids sat like a bump on a log. Upper management was seen as evil, and they felt like peons—complete one-eighty—now we were a team.

"What is a designated hitter?" Those were the words from Big R to Max Carlo at the second practice outside.... All the kids were huddled up....

"Max tells us all about that position?" Big R had him stand up in front of his peers. Coach had his watch right in front of his eyes—timing him down to the second.

"Go, tell us..."

Max went into rattling off the DH spot.

"Time—nice job...Philip your next—tell us about catcher..."

He rattled off all he knew about catchers catching ....

“Nice.” Then pointed right at Mike, “Tell us all about your greatest game.”

“What? What... Why me?” Mike voiced back....

“Okay, tell us anything you would like.” Now for the record, nearly all the kids would talk amongst themselves. But I believed, and told Coach, we needed the kids to talk more.... He asked, “What do you suggest”

I said, “Have all the kids talk about baseball, for five minutes....”

Nearly fifty practices later, every single player, from the non-talkers to the ramblers talked and talked.... I am a firm believer in kids who speak. We get the quiet ones to pop their heads out of their shells and it worked.

Mike was proof, and just like the Life cereal commercial. “He likes it. He likes it.” Mike really could talk it up—just needed encouragement and we all gave it to him. Some we had to limit their time, they were chatter boxes. Our team was talking.... And that is the way we started and ended every practice—a few minutes, for random players to speak—developing skills. Sure, a few were poked fun of, laughs were heard, but that's camaraderie at its finest....

Colton got in his five warm up pitches—

“TWO.... TWO....” Scott shared. A gun for an arm, nailed the imaginary runner and quick around the horn commenced—Ball back to Colton.

In the dugout, Coach K, and I, with Big R right next to us, came to the conclusion that if Colton gives up a big hit or a walk, then the switcheroo was on. Hawk for Colton. We would use Allen if we went into extra innings.

Colton looked at the sign—the first batter due up was the top of the lineup–one, two, three and possibly four.... cream of the crop....

Lead-off batter, the number one slot, was O for 3 –walk, strike out, and flyout to center.

“Look alive, Kevin. Look alive.” With that, Coach K scooted him back a few steps deeper in center—First pitch, of course, was always preplanned, fastball right around the plate. Colton got the sign and delivered a slower than normal heater. The batter swung,

“Foul ball.” Blue shared.

“Who’s up next after this kid?” Big R asked—

“Number two, he is one for three...”

"After that?"

"Dinger! He is three for three today."

Planning ahead and not just in the moment, Big R stressed to Coach K and me, over and over—first game, first home opener, Big R noticed neither K nor I were looking back to see what we had to do in the future. He never said a word to correct us in front of the kids. We won the game.

Next practice, he approached us, and explained that we all needed to plan out two or three batters, and even a few innings ahead, each, and every inning. "Ahead, look back...." I thought, genius.... Coach Jones, previously, always was reactive. Never proactive... "Proactive—that's the way we roll." Big R shared with the two of us....

I'll never forget Coach K's reaction— "A ton has changed since I played high level baseball in college, it ran like this—in my teenage years, late seventies, it was the coach who basically was the drill sergeant. Everything flowed through him. Right now, today Big R is funneling responsibility down to us, and holding us accountable...and I love it."

"Glory days!" I elbowed him...

"Yes, college ball was amazing..." We both gave the nod.

"Hawk.... Phillip.... bullpen, get a few more throws in."

"Yes, Coach Russell" They jogged down and warmed up proceeded....

Colton again, got the sign... two was given, Scott dragged his hands in the dirt—nothing to hit.... Batter chased it— "Strike two!" Ump gave out the 0 and 2 sign—Scott then gave a fastball, touched the top of his helmet—meaning high. Pitch was on its way, and it was like a trajectory we had never seen. Scott had to jump out of his stance, leap to his right, like a frog, mitt hand extended way up there—then THUD!!!!

"Just a bit outside..." I looked to my left...Carson, our third string catcher uttered those famous words...

"Yes, it was...."

Big R gave me the look, like where was that from... "Bend, bend." I was thinking Colton was getting tired, and it was evident now—two more balls were delivered, full count—

"Ball four." Ump pointed down to first....

"Time Blue—time." Big R shared with the Ump—then pointed to Coach K, "Hawk, let's get him in..."

Big R walked out to the mound, infield was all in—a few pats on the back were given to Colton, a few handshakes, and Coach took the ball from him. Hawk was on his way in.... Colton on his way out—making eye contact, gave each other high fives. All the kids in the dugout were outside the fence, each one shaking hands with forty-five.

"One heck of a game.... Nice job brother.... Awesome performance..." Kids relayed around him. Then I overheard, "Nice job, son. Nice job." It was Mr. Aries at the fence. After the kids settled down, he gave his two cents—one proud father-son moment....

"Strikes.... Strikes.... Throw strikes...." Big R exchanged with Hawk—Big R was never afraid to face a challenge head on. He exemplified that with all the players— "If we lose, or win, we give it 100%...." A few warmup pitches—Ump pointed to Hawk. Game on.

"Play is at two...." Keenan shouted out.... Joey followed him up with, "Hawk we got your back.... We got you!!"

The batter took his position, he was one for three, two strikeouts, and a double down third base line.

"Franky—your way.... Jason your way..." Coach K hollered, which moved Jason, who was now playing left field over a few steps and in a step....

Hawk came to his stretch, and of course, you can guess by now, fastball right down the middle.... Hawk glanced over, Keenan over towards third a tad, Joey would cover—batter had quick hands.... nothing worth reporting as far as a lead goes—with the delivery.... POP.... like striking a deep chord on a bass.

"Strike one!" Blue called....

Scott now was glancing over to first and noticed the runner lackadaisically walking back to first.... Scott again threw down the one and hit the outside of his thigh, then blurted out, "Let's go Danny...."

Hank, took to his stretch, Danny holding him on—a little more than three feet, not a steal lead, but a lead to extend him to third on a deep gapper to any location.... Danny gave the nod.... Ball was a little outside.... Scott took the ball, shifted his weight to his right, bent his left knee down, in a squatted position, and rifled the ball to Danny—

Receiving the ball, we had caught the runner with his head down, and standing straight up....

"Back.... Back...." First base coach called out.... With an attempt to get back, his weight was on his back heels. Danny looked the ball in, with a sweeping motion applied the tag at the top of the runner's attempt at a headfirst slide back....

"Out!" Called the umpire, as he gave the thumbs up motion and jerked back....

Instantly I heard, "No... No... No...." from the opposing bench. They were not thrilled at all—there was that word again.... NO....

"Outstanding, Scott!" I blurted out.... "Outstanding..." This was not Scott's first rodeo. In game three, the same chain of events took place. Only this time, Danny was not ready.... Scott had never thrown down to first at all. We practiced it. We drilled it. But it had never taken place....

Big R trained him to throw out the first baseman's name, to prepare him and be ready.... Danny's left thigh was bruised up for a few days, for he took it square in the thigh that game. Runner would have been out; Danny was just not ready.... Following that game, and all games...Big R with us coaches, had to follow through on the repetition of being ready. Think. Prepare. Anticipate.... and a code word always helps—Big R told Scott to use the first baseman's name—but look at the pitcher when saying it. No one would ever pick up on it. They think you're cheering your pitcher on.... It worked like a charm the second time.... and today was that second time.... we were one for one—

"Works every time," Klaus looked at me. It was awesome to witness.

"One out—play is to first..." Kids held up their fingers.

Hank got the ball, and now was facing the batter in a full windup position, no more stretch.... Because no one was on. It was an amazing inscription in the scorebook, 2 to 3 for the out.... Pretty cool to see it on paper, too. The count was one and one—

"Franky be ready.... Keenan, you, too...." Coach K shouted.... The pitch was just inside.

"Ball two..." Ump shared.

Hawk took a slow, deep breath, looked in—fastball down the middle.

"Foul ball.... foul ball." With that the Umpire stood there, looked to his left and looked to his right—

"Coming.... Here you go Blue." Sweats was right there, and realized ump had zero baseballs. Instantly he reacted and handled the situation.

"Here you go, sir." Sweats handed him a few.

Entering the dugout, "You're on it!" A few kids shared with Sweats.

Hawk got the sign, curve ball, he made the delivery and just like we planned, craaaacccckkkkkk, a line drive, a two-hopper between Keenan's right and Franky's left— Keenan made an excellent snag, was about to make a turn to throw....

"Eat it....no play..." His fellow players shared.... Keenan jogged the ball in.

"Dinger, Coach...dinger...." I shared with Big R......" He replied, "Next batter generated a few weak hits. Let's take it for the team."

"One out, plays at second. Plays at second." Infielders chatted it up.

"Scott, take the bat out of his hands." Big R voiced out, meaning walk the batter. The batter was three for three; went long, a double and triple—this young man was a player.

Scott told the umpire that we are intentionally walking this batter—"Take your base!" Ump pointed down to first....

"Oh, come on.... Can't get you out...." Fans shared, followed up by a few boooooooos....

First and second with one out sounded better than a tie game or worse, down by one run.... Big R, and all of us trusted our fielders.... "Any base.... any base.... one out, one out." Fielders shared with each other.

Next batter due up was one for two, a looper to left field, a walk, dribbler to Joey on second—nothing major. Big R liked our chances.

"Joey your way, Arnie look alive," bullhorn in effect for Coach K. "It never fails, nor does it ever need charging or new batteries." He said to me, with a smirk on his face. We laughed.

"Strikes Hawk! Strikes..." Big R volleyed his way.

Fastball as usual—this time, the kid was ready, I think the other team was on to us... it has happened before. Fastball in and a missile was launched....

Craccccckkkkkk.... the meat of the bat, this time paid off for the batter. He socked it deep to right center.

"OSCAR!!" Bench called out—

Runners were off to the races. Joey ran out.... Hawk took up his position behind third base.... The cutoff man drill was now live and in full effect.... Kevin, in an all sprint, headed to his left. Angle was great, but he bobbled the ball picking it up—it happens......causing the third base coach to send the runner.

"Third, third......" Fans, bench, and infield shifted gears ....

"Go. Go. Go." Other fans were cheering out......

The third Base coach waved the kid on to home and extended a single into a double. First base runner was now rounding second, heading to third. The hitter made his turn for second. Joey got a perfect bullseye to the chest from Kevin. He swiveled, threw a beam over to Franky at third, that pulled him off the bag....

Keenan hovering around second base yelled out, "TWO.... TWO.... TWO..." Franky with a dart to Keenan, nailed the runner for the second out.

If you had ever seen an old throwback Steven Seagal movie, non-stop action, well, you were living that scene now. I had never witnessed a ball go from 8 to 4 to 5 and to 6, with runners all trying to advance......

"Time...." Keenan called out.... Blue held up his hands...

Tie game. 6 to 6—wow what a regional game this was–the best of the best was shining through. "WOW!!!!" I looked over and I saw Greg and Steve giving each other high fives—yes, a run scored, but our bench had never seen ball movement like that before, when it mattered the most.... Our players loved it...

"Zero to zero," Little Timmy shared, and all his teammates pointed right at him—

"Let's go..." Big R with a smile, a shake of his head, and munching on sunflower seeds, glanced over to me, and gave me the two thumbs up.... Action was a complete understatement. It was the value of gold on the field—it was priceless to witness. The play, the kids' footwork, the calls on the field, and the backups by the fielders.... To outsiders, it may look chaotic, but to us, we played the way we practiced.

"Two outs...Two outs..." Hawk got the ball—took another deep sigh—Due up next was the number five hitter—he was one for two. Single, walk, and dribbler to first....

"Plays at one.... plays at first.... batter.... get the batter...." Kids shared.

Hawk took to the stretch—one peep over to third.... hurled in a fastball—

"Foul ball...." Claps took over the dugout....

Pitcher to the stretch, looking over, a little bit bigger lead—Franky scooted over.... runner faking to run. The delivery was deep in the dirt—Scott quick on his feet, shoveled to his right, and on one bouncer, brought his knees in, landed on his knees, brought both hands and glove in, crunched over and took the one bouncer off the protective chest hardware.

"Nice block, Scott!!!" Keenan shouted out.

Hawk got the call again, fastball, this time it was high...

"Ball high." Blue shared—held up one and two— "One ball, two strikes." Shared in his deep voice.

This time, Scott threw down a fist, or changeup, dangling his glove off his left knee to protect the sign.... Hank took his stretch, looked over, nothing major. Same clown routine going on, to distract him.... Left leg up, change up on the way. This time it was inside, Scott had to scoot over again. "Ball two...." Ump shared with us all. Quickly it turned to full count—Pointer finger down, and he touched the top of his head, Hawk knew the call and whisked a pretty fastball, down the plate, about chest high...batter was late. Wiiiiiiffffffffff.

"Strike three." Blue shared—-

Scott pointed right at Hawk. Hank's fist pounded the inside of his glove, over and over. Amazing inning.... and a new game... which means new strategy.... Leadership from Big R always flowed from start to finish.

As the kids ran off the field, the announcer said, "Let there be light...." The switches were thrown, and the stadium lights were flicked on.

"New game boys. Zero to zero." Big R shared with them, and patted Hawk on the back....

Top of the 8th

"Coaching is making men do what they don't want, so they can become what they want."

~Tom Landry

Scott took off his helmet, sat down next to me, and took a swig of Gatorade that Sweats handed him. Heavy breathing. Sweat was pouring down his face, grimy, dirt-filled hair, and with a smile said, "Thanks, Coach.... Thanks for all the drills. It paid off, could have been 7 to 6 them...instead it's zero to zero." Music to my ears.

To hear a young man say thank you, is a testimony to our team's love of small ball, discipline, and a massive tip of the cap to all our players. From OSCAR, to keeping the ball in front, to quick feet, to bullseye, to communication—that inning exemplified our epicenter.... that being a core unit.

I stood up and walked over to Big R. "Three for three, two for three, one for three and two for four." He gave me the nod. Started clapping his hand, and said, "Coach K, aggressive, aggressive–in a smart way." K gave him the nod, and the two took their positions at the corners.

Kevin's last at bats were, single, bunt, single. He is having an amazing game. Batting .1000 for the day. Big R gave him the sign to swing away. Nothing in his box of magic tricks was needed. Bruno was on deck—

"You've got this, Kev!" Bench hollered out.

Not a single kid was sitting down other than Hank. His arm was wrapped with towels...adding more insulation, with his throwing arm inserted in a team jacket. Sitting in the corner, swigging some hydration, and swirling his feet around in a circular motion—with a Cliff Bar in his hands.... Kids need to eat—plus it was getting late, as well. Not a fast game. Kinda long, at this stage. There was a ton of action on both sides of the dugouts. Kids were up for the challenge, and it was apparent.

"Strike one," Blue threw out. Followed by ball one, and ball two.

"Pitch, follow through," The opposing coach shared with the mound. "Relax, don't force it." Followed up.

Kevin dug in. Getting close to a hitter's pitch—two and one.

"Ball three." Blue held up 3 and 1—Big R gave him the swing away, three for three, who wouldn't—Batter was seeing the ball well, so why not allow him to do what was natural today. Sure enough, a slower than normal fastball was tossed in, instantly I knew Kevin was going to make contact—Crrrraaaccckkkkkk!!!! Kevin drove it, again, over the second baseman's head–cling, clack, ping, pang...The dugout fence was singing a tune, a strong tune.... a disturbing sound, the sound of rattling the fence profusely.

“Dugout etiquette, guys!” I looked over and there was Taylor, backup center fielder, “Don’t make us look like fools. We can cheer and scream, but nothing to smear our name.”

Leadership at its finest—months back, when we were handing out the uniforms, Big R told the kids, “When you wear this, you represent all of us...who we are, as an individual, as a team, and as a community—remember your last name is on the back. You can't see it, but others do. We want to be known as a team, and that's why our team logo is on the front......” That moment, Taylor stepped up and reiterated the team etiquette.... very cool to witness, he never said stop, no, quit—he just said, “Dugout etiquette.” Two words were enough.

Big R and I made eye contact—we looked over to the opposing bench, again two players were in their bullpen. Pop! Pop! Pop! could be heard. Lefthander, too.

An exchange would soon take place....

Big R took to his signs. Touching nose, belt, chest, both elbows, swing away motion, then followed up with landing his hands on both knees—the steal was on. Kevin was picked off in the first inning, but that was in the past. “Be a goldfish!” A *Ted Lasso* reference always got the kids laughing. Coach K used that line. Then I did, then Big R, then the whole team.... What’s done is done.... We can always reflect after the game, but forget mishaps and move on.

Bruno was two for three, single, single, and strike out.... Max was on deck—Big R made contact, “You've got this, Bruno, you've got this...” Gave him the signs, and the last one was a double fist pull back—meaning take this one. Pitcher came to his stretch, Kev had a nice lead, not overreaching but an extra half step...

“Back, back.” K shouted out.

“Safe.” Ump right there......Kev took his lead again. “Back! Back! Back!” K shouted again.

“Safe.” Blue again in a good position.... Kevin took one more half step. Pitcher at the stretch, this time his knee went past halfway, past his waist.

"Going! Going! Going!" The other team yelled out.... Bruno took the pitch, "Strike." The ump called—catcher had an awesome reaction, and glove to hand transaction, he released the ball—but it was a low throw, two-hopper.... feet first, and to the center of the bag.... a stolen base.

"Safe." Second base ump shouted.

Pitcher took the ball, and his stretch— "Swing away, swing away." Big R gave the motion, followed up with "Kevin, no outs. Be smart."

Kids all on their feet in the dugout. The bench was lined with sunflower bags, orange, green, red, and blue tiny Gatorade bottles flooded the wooden bench.... in a curved line from one end to nearly Hank's spot.... Kids were loving this, they were all in.

The pitch, "Ball." Blue held up one and one....

"Kev, be ready...." Big R motions.

Kevin took a little bit of a lead—the hurler took to his stretch, and like a stick figure throwing, the ball sailed right over the catcher's head....

"Go! Go!" Big R shouted to Kevin.

"Clang," the ball hit the fence, and rolled around the bottom of the backstop.... "Down, down..." But no throw was attempted, the catcher ate the ball....

"Play at home or first." Kids shouted to each other....

Bruno dug in, and with the count two and one—another hitter's pitch was due his way.

"Drive it.... drive it..." Bench howled out.

The ball zoomed in, and a drive right down third base was given. This ball was hit with authority to the hot corner, he was in a few steps, looked the ball in, catching it about chest high—Kevin nearly a quarter of the way down the line to home.

Big R hollered out, "Back! Back! Back!" He dove headfirst, simultaneously with one step and a jump. Third baseman leaped, extending the glove to the base of the bag–

"Safe.... Safe...." Blue hollered out, just by a hair, or the tip of his batting gloves, Kevin was safe at third....

"One out. One out...." Kids in the field hollered out....

"Time Blue, time..." Opposing coach pointed his way...the switch was on......Left-handed pitcher entered the game. One out, man on third, and our DH was due up. Max was 1 for 3, pop out, line drive to second, and first at bat had a single to left field. Max was seeing the ball well, making great contact. Even though he only had one hit, or .333, he still was making contact....

Big R looked in at Max, Keenan was on deck.... He walked over to me at the edge of the dugout, as the pitcher got his warmups in— "Get Ian warming up, he will bat for Danny if it is called for." Ian was a starter last year. Danny at first was just better. He grew a few inches over the past year, his bat was better. Ian, was the hitter we could lean on, during the season, when need be. He got his playing time at numerous positions, got his cuts in too—over the past fifteen games. He either got in, or pinched hit, or pinched ran as the game called for and he always delivered.

"Ian—get warmed up." I said.

"Yes, sir."

He knew instantly what to do. Ian was excellent at left-handed pitchers. Even though he batted right, he for some reason picked up the ball better than others. Coach K realized that weeks ago, and we always used it to our advantage, hidden gem and we found it.

Max dug in, pitcher now could face Kevin on third with his back—nothing fancy, Kev standing in foul territory...

"Contact.... contact.... swing away." Big R shared and pointed at Max, again giving him the hit away motion.

"Strike one..." Blue shared.

"Nice cut, wait for it..." Coach K threw down to Max....

"Strike Two...."

"Nice cut.... head in and drive it."

A pitch of all pitches was thrown in, a curveball with a nice snap, headed right down the pipe, and broke inside Max's swing....

"Strike three..." Blue hollered out....

Keenan gave Max a low five, as they walked by each other to their spots—batter's box and dugout. "Keenan, drive him in...." Kids still on their feet voiced out.

"Two outs.... Play's at first.... Play's at first..."

KJ looked down to third. Shortstop, second, and first basemen were all playing in. The opposing coach understood that everything was on the table.

"Drive it." Big R, shared.

"Ball one." Blue said—a full count followed very quickly.... you could sense this pitcher, like others we have seen, liked to work fast....

"You've got this kid...you've got this...." Our bench cheered him on.

Keenan, crowded the plate, in just a smidgen. "Ball four..." Blue pointed down to first....

"Two outs.... two outs.... play at first or second...." Infielders passed around.

"Time, Blue," I said, and I darted to home plate to tell the umpire that a change was taking place.

"Now batting, number thirty-seven, Ian Rivers." Again, P.A. announcer was in the game.

Yeppers, two Rivers on the team—cousins.

Ian took his place in the batter's box, looked down to third—like a broken record, Big R gave the swing away motion.... Keenan had a good lead at first.

"Batter! Get the batter." Opposing coaches yelled out. Like a preemptive strike, something so organized, well planned out was about to take place.

Fans were on their feet. Pitcher took to his stretch, the ball whisked in and a drive to center field was underway. One pitch, one at bat, and a run scoring RBI was created. Great hit. Kevin made his way into home.... Keenan over to second... We were up 7-6. Ian came through. The right call, at the right time, delivered.

"Two outs. Play at third, second or first." Infielders voiced out.

Big R was in a louder than normal clap. He was so pumped down at third, his clap echoed throughout the ballpark. Our bench and fans were going crazy. Momentum shifted to us, up by one run....

Joey was due up next—having a solid game at second and at the plate—two for four. Pitcher peered over to second and first—rifled a strike in there, followed up by strike two, a ball and a massive cut by Joey.

“Strike three.” Blue went into his left arm out, right arm pulled back for the third out. Lefty on the mound, had the right-handed batters' numbers, but Ian came through...

As the kids all stood outside the dugout, ready to retake the field–Coach K was in the middle— “Trust each other. Talk it up. Do Your Jobs!!!” He began to clap vigorously over and over. “Let's go.”

“Max—get warmed up buddy.” Big R pointed to him. He was our back up, to the back-up relief pitcher. Strong arm. Good placement, with nothing over the top—he threw strikes.

“Phillip, get him ready.”

“Yes sir, Coach.” Phillip was getting his steps in. They took their position down at the bullpen.

“Nice hit, Ian.... Nice hit....” I could hear his family exchange words as he took his position out at first.

What I noticed before taking the field, was an exchange between Danny and Ian—an exchange of teammates, rooting each other on. “WHAT A HIT!” Danny welcomed him in the dugout with a two-step jump and chest pump—very cool to see. Competitors cheered each other on—as they took the field, Danny was the last one to sit down. He walked down the dugout, and gave each kid and the coaches a fist bump—and the last one was Sweats, he gave him a high five.

Bottom of the 8th

“The most important thing in communication is hearing what isn’t said.”

~Peter Drucker

“Two for three, one for three, one for three.” I fed Big R the next wave of batters.

“After that?”

“One for three.” Big R smacked his left hand with a fist....

“Be ready Franky. Keenan be ready.” Coach K shared with the kids, then into, “Your way last time, Bruno....” With the faux bullhorn to his face.... All the kids gave the nods....

“Get two.” Scott rifled the ball down to second. A quick whisk around, with the ball back to Hank on the mound. He took a deep breath and knew what to do... Fastball—Franky was even with the bag....

“Ball high,” Ump called—

Which followed up with, “Foul ball.” With a loud clunk to the back stop.... nice cut, but got under it. Scott called for a change up, two fastballs, so it was followed up nicely, as Scott swiped the dirt on the ground. Meaning keep it down. Well, the next pitch got away from Hank, as if he released it too late. It took a small bounce about an inch in front of home plate—

“Ball...” Blue called. Scott scooped it up, 2 and 1 held up in the air–

“Strikes, strikes....” Hank took his wind up, made a piercing fastball down the middle—POP! The ball exploded off the bat, a deep poke to right field—Bruno was right there to receive the ball on a two bouncer....

Gotta love, low, line drives, just within three feet over the second baseman's head. Joey, by no means, was going to get that one. Keenan hustled over to second, took his ready position—Bruno threw it in....

“No outs! Play’s at second or first.” Kids all shared with each other.

I looked at Coach K, and he pointed to his watch—meaning close for the call to get Max into the dugout, from the bullpen.

“Few more.” I heard Big R state.... meaning a few more pitches for Hank and a few warmups for Max. Now Max was our DH, that would be addressed later...Right now concentrate on getting off the field.

Dugout was about half standing, quarter pacing and a quarter sitting down. If a photographer took a photo from last year at this same moment, you'd see ninety-nine percent sitting on the bench. Today, a quarter were sitting, and they were interchangeable—like Whac-A-Mole.

Up, down, up, up, down, down, never the same click of kids huddled in a tight circle. All the kids were constantly moving.

"No outs.... No outs..." Followed up by, "Keenan be ready." Coach K scooted him over a few steps towards second...anticipating a steal was on. Hawk took the ball—Ian was holding him, not a natural position, but one that worked. The delivery was made, Scott had called a fastball this time, surprise....it just is the way it was. POP!!!! As if a secret had been let out. The batter sat back and drove this to deep right center—just outside of Jason's reach. He and Kevin were mad dashing for the ball—

"Got it! Got it!" Kevin called out—Base runner was turning for third.

"Oscar!" Keenan took off.

"Left...Left..." Franky got him in position. With his bare hands, Kevin picked up the ball. "Third! Third!" The players called out. Runner was about halfway, when the opposing coach held up two hands—the baseball stop sign was in full force. Kevin made contact with Keenan, who pivoted, made a beeline for third—this time, it was way left, out of reach of Franky. As rehearsed, there was Hank, in position to back up the throw. The play I just witnessed, was not a starter on the mound, not our ace by any means—a relief pitcher, following through on drills we had done months ago—Hank was one for one—not once had he had to perform this, and that day it worked as scripted.

"Get Max please, Sweats..." A nod, then a burst down the line.

"Time.... Time Blue..." Hank knew his time was up—Big R made his way to the mound, placed his right hand out. Hank placed the ball in and jogged off the mound....

"Nice game, son," I heard his dad call out....

As Max made his way in, head up high, all the players were there to greet him with open arms. "Nice job, Hawk...." was expressed his way. Instantly, Klaus handed him a cup of water, and his jacket— "Thanks, buddy..." Without hesitation, he spun around and turned and planted his face against the chain-link, standing there with his teammates, and said, "You've got this kid.... Max.... Maximum effort...."

"Five pitches!" Blue chimed out.... Big R made his way into the dugout....

"One for three, one for three, and two for four..." I conversed with him—strategy was the name of the game. "Anything extra about them?" Coach K, right along with us, asked. "Was in a pickle, stole second, and #9 hitter is a switch hitter, got a hit last at bat, awful at lefthanded."

With that, Coach K took to the imaginary bullhorn, "Franky!" with a hand motion moved him a step to third.... "Keenan!" Moved him out and towards the middle. "Joey!" He moved him to second and closer to the infield grass. "Watch two. Watch two." Max took his warmups, looked over to first, Ian holding him on. Then looked to his right, Joey hitting the inside of his glove....

Scott squatted down, gave the sign, and as Big R predicted, they had a spy on the other team—not really, just knew a fastball was coming. Max picked up his left foot, and made an amazing stride, for a relief pitcher, and tossed in a vicious change up.

"Strike one." Blue called out.

Batter was so far out in front, a few hats in our dugout fell off. "Holy cow." I heard Hawk say. Big R told Scott no more fastballs on first pitch. Proven to be effective, change it up—unless we tell you.

Lead at second was pretty good. "No outs," kids all shared. "Third, second or first." followed up. Max got the sign, hurled in another change up...

"Strike two." Blue held up a fist and bunny ears—

"Nice, Max. Nice...." Fans were cheering.... Both sides had been on their feet and cheering nearly the entire game. Dads were pacing along the fence line, even grandparents were giving a few hoots and hollers. Baseball in its final hour.

"Contact...stay back." The other team gave a few pointers to the batter.

Max dug his foot in a little more than usual around the rubber, came to the stretch, and whisked in a fastball.

"Foul ball." Blue shared.

Again, looking to first and second, Max threw in another fastball. This time the batter smacked a hit within two feet of Ian at first. It was not a routine play by any means. It was hard, a few bounces. Holding the runner on, getting in position after the throw, he made an athletic move to his right. Max, seeing what was transpiring, made an instant reaction and headed for first. The ball took a horrible bounce off the lip of the grass, jolting up about three feet. Ian's chest took the impact of the ball, keeping his body in front, sacrificing his limbs and torso. The ball landed dead in front of him. Going to his knees, he underhanded the ball over towards first. Max in full speed made a backwards catch, preventing the ball from passing, extending his right leg.

"OUT!!!!" Blue shared....

Cheers erupted in our dugout, and throughout the crowd—it was an amazing play. One that worked effectively, through the process of "run it again," in practice.

Nearly four months ago, Ian, Danny and a few other players were introduced to the pitching machine.... "Not hard, Sweats!"

There on the field, between first and home, and pitcher's mound and baseline, a pitching machine was aimed in the grass.

"Okay guys let's do it." Big R expressed....

"Do what?" Ian said.

"Take one for the team... hahaha. Just kidding, keep it in front of you." Big R chuckled.

Minutes into warmups Coach K took the outfielders. I took pitchers over for a drill. All we could hear was, "Keep it in front of you, nice job...run it again..."

I looked over, Sweats was feeding the pitching machine...about fifty mph was set, and the kids were receiving routine ground balls at first.... then placing the ball in the bucket, no throwing. Then Coach said, "Dial it up..." Fifty became sixty, then seventy, then eighty, all the infielders were taking ground balls. Move in, move back, to the left, to the right." Big R shared with them—this exercise took place nearly once a week, about fifteen minutes. Everyone got in at least ten turns.

Ian, a backup first baseman, made that play because of constant coaching, constant action, and constant repetition. "Do it again," paid off....

"One out, one out...." Kids all shared with each other—

“Up the middle last time, K.” He gave me the nod, bullhorn to the mouth, “Kevin...” With two hands, he gave him the come in motion, then two hands up to stop.

“Batter, Max.” Big R dished out.

Max peeked to third–nothing fancy, batter took a few cuts.

“Let's go, kid. Let's go, Max.” Bench voiced out.

Max again, threw in a strange pitch for the team–fastball. Good rip.

“Foul ball.” Blue shared....

A little bigger lead on third, Franky grazing the bag, Joey holding at second, within a few steps.... Curve outside, was on the way—Scott had to dive to his right and blocked the ball.... “Nice save...one...seven.... nice save.” Teammates barreled out. Ump held up one and one—

Max peered over. “Max it out! Max it out!” Franky shared with him.

Fastball again, crack, this one again was hit up the middle, but Max was right there. He instantly knocked the ball down; it rolled down the mound—batter was off to the races. Max bent down, and grabbed the ball, but it was rolling. He missed the first attempt. He lifted his head up, grabbing the ball. This time, he picked it up, looked to third, runner was not going, and with authority threw it to Ian on first. It was close.

“Safe...” Blue called out. Ian did not have his foot on the bag...missed it by a camel hair...Ump gave the motion of two hands to his right, in a sweeping motion.... pulled off the bag. Bases loaded.

“Forget it.... batter. Get the batter.” Fielders chatted it up— “Any base.”

“Time blue...time....” Opposing coach walked out to home plate. With that a pinch hitter was entering the game. We hadn’t seen him yet. And the last batter was zero for three, with a walk.

Good timing if you ask me from a coaching perspective.

“Home.... keep it in front.” Coach K used the faux bullhorn. Then muted it. Then flipped it on, and with his right hand to his mouth blasted out, “MARTY!!!” He pointed to Franky on third and Ian at first—squeeze maybe on.... “Keenan.... cover...” Nods all around.

Max knew what MARTY meant; he was ready. Max took to his stretch, whisked in a fastball....

“Strike one” Blue called....

Fans were going crazy, on the home team side, “Go yard!” I heard—followed by “Dinger, rope it, get a hold of it.” Parents, and friends all cheering their team on—

Then I distinctly heard, “Max you've got ‘em.” I looked to my left and there was Little Timmy giving his two cents and chirping right along with his teammates. All were on their feet.... The bench was completely vacated—including K, Big R, and me—sardines lined the chain-link fence.

Scott put down another one, this time I could sense the inning starting to get out of hand. Max threw the heater down and in, skipping right past the edge of Scotts glove...

“Going, going, going....” Our bench screamed out. All the runners were advancing.

Scott had to run back about fifteen feet to the back stop, Max hustled in.... Scott threw his mask off, slid into the fence, picked up the ball, falling back he threw to Max hovering over home plate.

“Safe, safe.” Umpire giving the rapid safe motion over and over—dust clouds again seemed to find the field. 7-7 all tied up again. New game.

“One out...one out.... play is at home....” Scott halfway to the mound shared with his team. Count was one and one—it quickly turned to ball three— Big R looked at me and he said, “Bruno.”

Blue then shared, “Take your base.”

Big R popped out of the dugout, “Time blue, time....... BRUNO....” Big R tapped his right shoulder. Bruno came barreling out to the mound. Big R walked out, took the ball from Max, and Max darted off to right field. The old switcheroo was on, something you might see in little league—but it was an all-hands-on-deck situation. We didn’t want to use our closer, yet. Extra innings, if need be, we would use him—Big R shared with us. The game was close, but we were hitting the ball well today.

“Five warm-up pitches.” Blue shared with Bruno—

Now, for the record, Bruno was one of the young men, that said he had never pitched before in his life. That night in the gym, with the wooden mounds, and makeshift rubber.... Bruno had an arm, just couldn't grasp the windup, or science behind the position—but he was athletic. POP! POP! POP! was heard that night. Big R and Coach K were convinced that with a little coaching, guidance, and mentorship from other pitchers, that, yes indeed, Bruno could be used as a pitcher. Weeks upon end, they worked with him, gave him the motion, gave him the insights and the mechanics, and they created a pitcher, not just any pitcher, but a pitcher we only use when needed.

It was around game five in the season, and we were up eight to one over a team. We brought Bruno in.... He pitched a shutout inning, one inning we determined was enough, maybe two if need be. Five or eight batters was enough for Bruno. We put him in four more games, and he did terrific. This time, it would be the same...

Bases loaded, one out—

"Two Ks.... left field double, too." I shared with Coach K and Big R.

"Jason, be ready." He held up his glove and gave a smile.

Bruno looked in, and Scott gave him one.

"Strike one." Blue called out—

Scott again gave one and touched his helmet... "Can of corn...can of corn." Coach K blurted out. The batter took a great cut but got underneath it. A high fastball has that effect...

"I got it, I got it." Keenan called out....

"Home.... home...." Bruno took up his position behind home plate....

"Two hands, two hands...." I heard a fan share. Keenan on a back pedal, about two feet into left field, looked the ball in, and smothered it—Runner on third, faked running in, trying to get Keenan to throw over. But he knew better. He simply ran the ball in and called time. Umps held up two hands.

"Dinger last time..." I expressed this to both coaches....

Coach K stepped out, "Jason, Kevin, Bruno!" He gave them the backup signal, following it up with, "Keep it in front.... Keep it in front...."

Big R clapping, making eye contact with Bruno, giving him the I believe in you signal.... Bruno peered in. Scott gave him the one, touched his helmet—He whisked a ball, which instantly was foul tipped, drifting high and out beyond the backstop....

Head-to-head—batter was three for three today, a gifted young man.... Bruno looked in, Scott gave him one, and touched his helmet, again—

Bruno never once glanced at any of the runners—focusing in on only the hitter, just like Big R told him...

Again, "Foul ball." Umpire hitting the top of his left fingers....0 and 2....

"Nothing...nothing..." Big R shared again.

Scott again gave him a fastball and his hand hit the dirt, indicating keep it down.... Crackkkk, it was a nice hit up the middle, or so I thought it was. Joey was in position, made a dart to his right, backhanded the ball into glove, and flipped the ball over to Keenan for the third out.

Backhand—Joey on his toes, made a great play. It looked effortless, but ninety days ago it was hard, hard on all the kids. In the gym, which carried to the practice field, Big R worked on the backhand over and over. Explaining that we want to line our body up, keep the ball in front—back hand is routine when rehearsed over and over. With the fungo bat, working with the infielders, Big R would, with precision placement, work on the ready position. Rotation, foot movement, and throwing motion. Cocking the arm back, and throwing, not aiming, but throwing. Joey ate the ball up, what should have been a single up the middle turned into a third out...

All the kids were out of the dugout, again it was a new game...zero to zero.

Top of the 9th

"Real leadership is about transforming limitations into possibilities."

~Robin Sharma

"Folks, what a game we have today." I heard the P.A. announcer go into his toolbox of words. Then shared, "Split the pot results are here...if you have number 77, then you have just won the grand prize of three hundred and seventy-five dollars. So, come on up, and collect your winnings.""

7 + 7, what does that equal? I was thinking. Instantly I thought of Pete Rose, who else is famous for 14. And another thing, at Great American Ball Park, where I love to go, the two stacks in center field, each have seven bats wrapped around the top of each column—7 plus 7 is 14...tribute to Pete Rose in a discrete fashion, kinda like the hidden Mickeys at Disney.

"We got this..." I heard the kids say......

"What a game...what a game!" I heard a parent just outside the dugout share. This was Clash of the Titans.

"Timmy, Chucky, Juan, get warmed up. Start some running." Big R shared with the boys. "Trey! Grab a bat. You are in for Bruno." He spun around, clapping his hands, and with a huge smile on his face rattled off, "Phillip! You and William down to the bullpen. Get ready Bobby!" Instantly the five boys took off.

Big R, Coach K and I stood in the corner— "Dedication will win this game. I can't thank you both enough for your discipline." Big R gave us both a handshake, followed up with, "Do your job." He and K took off for first and third.

Kevin was the leadoff hitter, and today he was three for three having a monster of a game. The infield felt off key. They were deeper than normal. They knew Kevin had a few zingers. Like Big R said, "We use it all." "Let's go Marty! Let's go." Big R shared with Kevin.

Right away Kevin knew exactly what to do—take the first pitch, then follow that up with a great bunt.

Pitcher released the ball, a little high.

"Ball one..." Blue shared.

"Marty, you've got this." Big R rehashing the signals again. He went to square off the release, but pulled back. The ball was high again.

"Ball two..." Blue shared.

The sign was off, for the control was not there, plus Big R knew this was a hitter's pitch— "Swing away Kevin, swing away." Big R exploded his invisible bat.

"Watch for a bunt...." Opposing coaches called out....

The third baseman scooted in, and first mimicked his advancement. Ball was on the way—Crrrrraaaaaccccckkkkk!!! As Big R knew it, Kevin again drove the ball up the middle, just left of the short stop. "Four for four!" I shared with the dugout....

"What a hit... nice rip.... way to see it." All the kids were going nuts in the dugout.

"One play, one batter, one inning." I looked over and there was Alex sharing that with the whole team.

"Time Blue! Time. Juan you are in..." With Bruno on the on-deck circle... Big R shared, then approached the umpire at home plate, pointed to first, pointed for the switch, and the two players ran off, and on the field—Kev out and Juan in.

Coach K gave Juan a fist bump and went over a few tactics, pointing at the shortstop and towards Big R. All the kids welcomed Kevin in with high-fives. Sweats took his helmet and placed it in the box. Kevin spun to line up against the fence... "Come on Juan.... come on." He screamed out.

Big R looked at me, and shared, "T......Trey." He gave me the timeout symbol. left hand horizontal, right had vertical on top. The call was on. "Trey you are on deck..." I told him...

"Alright. Alright. Alright." I heard the kids say, once Trey was called up to bat next.

Juan stood on first, Big R stood at third, bent over with both hands on his knees—the steal sign was on—Bruno took a look down, got the sign, and heard "Drive it." Big R railed out—

Juan was not the fastest by any means, but he had an explosive first step, faster than any other kid on the team. In the gym, sprinting from one end to the other, Juan was fast out of the gate, all the coaches picked it. "There is our Brice Turang." Coach K said back in the earlier days. "We will use him well." Big R shared—numerous times, Juan pinch ran—he was nine for eleven stealing. Today would not be any different. Our chances were very good to get him over to second.

Pitcher took to the stretch—Peered over at Juan, who had a four-step lead.

“Back!” K hollered.... Ump right there, with the safe sign.

“Stay, stay.” Coach K hollered out .... The old fake throwback to pitcher was on, Juan held his position—ball eventually tossed over. Pitcher took his stretch again, Juan this time had a four and half step lead. The leg went right past mid-section.

“Going.... going....” Kids scrambled out. Bruno sitting back on the ball was ready and he drove it, drove it right over the third baseman's head. Juan kicked up a little dirt in his slide into second. He bounced right up, ready to take third....

“Time blue.... time...” Big R walked down, pointed to Trey and into the dugout....

“Timmy you are in! Get down to first.”

“No outs, play is at any base...” Kids in the infield shared with one another.

“Now batting #88, Trey Heckler...” Big R gave T the look of HIT IT....

Big R took his spot, Juan and Little Timmy had pretty good leads, maybe three steps, nothing to indicate a steal was on.... Pitcher took to his stretch, quick peek and hurled a fastball.

“Strike one.” Blue shared...

Big R again said, “Drive it.”

Trey got in a few more practice swings, really keeping his head down, and exploding through. Pitcher took his delivery, tossed in a pretty good curveball—instantly it was a barrel it up swing.... Contact was made, deep to right field. He didn’t crush it, but contact was made....

“Tag...Tag.” Big R hollered out to Juan....

“Halfway! Halfway!” Coach K expressed to Timmy....

The ball hung up in the air, he drove it deep, but the right fielder was in position to make the play. Second was out for a cut off.

“Go.... Go....” Big R shared with Juan.... he was barreling down the baseline, head down, and in control.... He slid in feet first, but no play was put on....

"Nice job, Trey...." Fans and teammates were celebrating as he sprinted off the field. "Way to move them over, Trey." Dugout said, high-fives all around. I could hear Mr. Heckler, "Way to drive it to the opposite field, son." Music to my ears. Trey indeed had a great hit. He got little playing time, but he always delivered when needed.

One day after practice, Trey's dad, Mr. Heckler walked with me from the field to the parking lot and shared that a few months back, after a day practice, Trey asked if they could set up a tee and a safety net in the basement. He went on to say, that he had never been asked that before, nor had Trey ever practiced on his own. Mr. Heckler said, "I wanted you to know how much this season means to him—your coaching style, the team's transition, and the team environment are truly remarkable. Trey is loving it."

You see, months ago, Big R stressed that we were limited on time. Take what you learn from here and practice with your dad, brother, mom, sister, neighbor, grandpa, and more importantly practice on your own. He had a catch phrase, "Character is what you do, when no one is looking." Trey set up a mock home plate, and placed the tee on the inside to pull, on top of to drive up the middle, and outside to drive to opposite field. All three stages he had been working on. Trey was the line leader, and other players set up a basement station, as well.... We never heard how many, but the rumor was somewhere around twenty kids imitated him and followed suit.

"One out..." Infielders shared....

"He's a bunter. He will square up." Again, talking it up in the field.

Big R and Coach K looked at each other. K hit the top of his left hand.... We all peeked over to the opposing bullpen, a southpaw was indeed warming up—could hear a few pops. Nothing major, but as the hooting and hollering died down, the ball hitting the mitt created an echo...

Keenan stepped out of the on-deck circle, Big R, again with his hands on his knees made eye contact—with the words, "Let's go Smitty..."

Smitty was another word for bunt.... Marty sometimes was obvious and if a batter was asked to bunt, a second code word was used. Runners got the sign. Keenan took some massive cuts, players on first and third. One out.... Both dugouts were on their feet, the crowd was on their feet. The pitcher glanced over. Juan was ten steps down third baseline in foul territory. The third baseman was just about even with the bag—the pitch was on. Juan took off, Little Timmy took off.

"Going, going, going..." The infield yelled out. They were caught off guard, and screamed, "Bunt! Home! Home!"

Practice makes perfect, and a perfect bunt was placed down first base line.... Pitcher landed on his left foot, so naturally he was pulled off the mound.... First baseman took two steps in, Keenan was exploding down the line.... Juan was high tailing it into home.... The pitcher had to make a great play, he did.... snatched the ball with his right hand, made an athletic move. Threw the ball sideways to the catcher at the plate, it was going to be close.

"Safe.... safe......" Blue called out......

The crowd was going ballistic.... Roars and cheers so loud, it was deafening, in an amazing way. Dugout players were on their feet, "We are up...we are up." I heard a few guys chatter.... It was so accelerating. A warm, Diet Coke sip was what I needed....

If a brush was ever needed by an umpire, today was the day. Quite the action all around the bases—Blue pulled out his little brush, butt to the pitcher, and swept away the debris—

"Juan, you the man......Nice job BIG J...." Kids smothered him in the dugout.

8 to 7 us and only one out.... runners at first and second. I was thinking if a game would ever be remembered, this is the one.

"Time Blue......time." Big R shouted down, "Chucky you are in...." The Chuckster took off down to first, switching out with Keenan as a pinch runner. As he headed in, one smother continued into another smother. Kids all rallied around Keenan— "What a bunt.... Nice placement kid..." Bench was chiming in all around.

"Time, Blue.... Time...." Opposing coach called out.... A call to the bullpen was underway. Good time for everyone to catch their breath.... The southpaw approached the mound, Blue was there and handed him the ball, and said, "Five."

"Now batting, #37 Ian Rivers." P.A. announcer identified the next batter. Ian had switched out with Danny on first base in the eighth inning, and drove a nice single up the middle.

"See the ball, hit the ball." Big R shouted out, again, some speed was on the bases.... Little Timmy was not a mile a minute like Juan, but was a wildfire. Big R touched his nose, chin, both ears, wiped his chest, bent over, touched both knees, and unleashed a massive mock swing to Ian.... "Drive it." The double steal was on. Aggressive was an understatement, plus Ian batted left-handed....

Pitcher looked over, nothing major, third baseman was even with the bag–just about five steps away, he was thinking steal. Timmy had about a four-step lead, Chucky about three. He took his delivery in.

"Going! Going! Going!" Other teams and fans shouted out–

Indeed, little Timmy was flying, looking like Tom Cruise in *Mission Impossible* on a rooftop.... He was galloping .... Chucky, too, was making a mad dash for second.

Pitch was on its way, Ian took a swing at it, WIFFFFFFFF....

"Strike one..." Blue shared, I thought the same thing. Caught Ian off guard. Curve ball inside, and he was thinking fastball. Catcher was nowhere near a good spot to make a throw down to third.... Too good of an inside curveball. Timmy and Chucky both advanced—

"Drive it." Big R again with cheers.

"Ball inside." Blue was still in motion and with zest 1 and 1 was held up.

Still just one out.... Timmy standing in foul territory, I heard Big R share— "Tag if it's deep...."

Next pitch was a nice four-seam fastball down the middle—Ian indeed got the barrel of the bat on the ball, driving it to center field. I think the player took an inch step to his left....

"Home...Home..." Man if they are calling home, he must have a good arm...

"Tag, tag." Big R said.

Timmy scooted back, took the set position facing home.... Catch was made in stride, "Go, goooooooooo!" On a line drive throw, no bouncer, but a line drive. Little Timmy was again off to the races, with a terrific leap forward, Timmy went into his headfirst slide, a car wash moment.... Catcher received the ball way off to his right, looked it in with two hands, and dove to his left, attempting a tag, but he was late....

"Safe.... Safe...." Blue called out......

Fireworks like crazy were all over the place, boos to wows, to amazing, to stomping feet on bleachers, to high fives. I could hear the other team kicking the chain link fences.... It was now 9 to 7 us....

Big R looked over his left shoulder— "Phillip! Is Bobby ready?"

"Few more."

"Okay, get him in the dugout and hydrate him up."

"Yes, sir."

"Two outs.... Play's, at first...." Infielders shared amongst themselves.

Joey was due up next, he had struck out last time— Joey took his spot at the plate. Again, Big R, coaching and managing this team with discipline, looked in and said, "Drive it.... launch it..." Joey wasn't seeing the ball too well today, was two for four, but his field work, now that was newsworthy. K used to say, "100% effort! That's all we ask." Joey gave it, day in and day out.

"Strike one...." Blue shared....

Crowd piped down a few. Our kids were still on their feet. Pitcher followed up with two balls and a strike.... Chucky was given the green light, on the next pitch.

"Going! Going!!!!" Kids yelled out.... No play at third. The batter, was the focus.

"Quick hands," Big R said again with a compacted swing, as he unleashed a ton of sunflower seed shells after his imaginary swing. I'm telling you what, birds are going to flock to third after this game—intense down there. Joey got his pitch, ripped hard to his left, second baseman playing deep in the hole, took the ball on a bounce.

"First." Kids yelled out.

Second baseman looked the ball in, and on a two-step skip, chucked the ball to first. End of the inning, out number three. But what an inning it was. The strength of each player was brought out and folks were witnessing what it means to have a good bench.

Bottom of the 9th

"Talent wins games, but teamwork and intelligence win championships."

~Michael Jordan

“Now pitching, William Carroll for the Titans.” The P.A. announcer shared. Then he went into something I had never heard. “Free hotdogs and burgers, come and get them.”

“Coach, you want one???” Sweats asked me.

I was quick with a reply. “No way!!! I wouldn’t miss this inning for the world.”

“Me either," he said.... Me either.”

“I wouldn’t have missed this game for the world.” Phillip then rattled off.

Huge smiles on all the boys' faces, quickly turned into extreme focus, with the next three batters due up—all were in tune. I leaned over, looked over to the third base fence, and there was Jimmy Olsen. Now, for the record Superman was nowhere in sight, but our hometown beat reporter/photographer was there gathering a few photos and jotting down a few notes.

I could never remember his name—we just called him Jimmy.

“There's Jimmy.” I heard one player say, then pointed over to his left. Kids loved when Jimmy came around. Everyone loves coverage. When Jimmy was around, then indeed it’s something newsworthy.

“You've got this Bobby! Which was instantly followed up with, “Come on four...four.” Fans extended a hearty welcome to Will—Bobby is what everyone referred to him as, and of course his number was #14....

“Two!” Scott called out—another quick around the horn was executed. Franky walked the ball in and handed it over. He leaned in, giving him a glove-to-the-back pat, and a few uplifting words.

The leadoff hitter, or the number four hitter in the lineup was one for three. Last at bat he hit a nice single to right. Coach K was quick to react, “Joey, be ready. Kevin.... Max.... Be ready.” Then he put his bullhorn down.

Big R shouted out to Bobby, “DIVIÉTETE!” Which was Spanish for have fun. He responded with “Sí, Señor!”

There were three words spoken at the try-outs, months ago now, EVERYONE BUNTS and GRADES!!!!

The motto of the team was everyone bunts, however the theme that Big R stressed right out of the gate was, "You can't bunt if don't have the grades to be here."

A few months back, Bobby approached Coach K and asked him if he could leave practice early, so he could get a little more studying done before a mid-term exam. Big R stressed grades—firm believer in baseball was second to school-work— "Of course Coach K said. After practice, myself, and Big R confronted Coach K— "Is Bobby okay, we saw him leave early?" I asked. "Of course. He needed more studying time and asked to leave." We all laughed, that is the mind-set of a student athlete. Turned out he got an A in Spanish that semester. Last year, Jones never hammered grades, he just said all kids need good grades, and that covered the subject.

In the dugout before the transition, Big R and I went over the next three batters with Scott—heater, heater, and curve.... those were the pitches to start off with. From there, we trusted Scott, maybe a little coaching if need be—other than that, Bobby and Scott worked well as a team.

"Strike one." Blue called out.

Bobby had an amazing stride towards home plate, something that gave him an extra pop that he didn't have at the beginning of the season. Coach K noticed that Bobby was naturally falling to his right more than normal. Bobby was fighting so hard to land square with home plate— "Who cares if it pulls you off to third. Your location, timing, and outcome work when you don't fight the cause." Those words rang true—he did look a little weird, landing to his starboard side, an analogy Coach K would use with him. Bobby was a master angler and loved to share with us his fishing tales.

"Ball high." Blue shared, then went into ball two....

"Don't aim!" Coach K emitted to Bobby.

Scott gave him another one down, and a massive swing was unveiled. With major contact.

"Foul Ball." Blue called out. Blue hit the top of his finger, and the ball exploded straight back into the backstop.

"Two and two," Umpire yelled out—again extending two sets of rabbit ears in the air for all to see.

"Joey, be ready." Coach using his bullhorn....

Pitch was on the way, and like we all thought, the batter undeniably created a poke to the right. This time, between Joey and Ian, with a powerful line drive, that landed in shallow right field. Trey exploded in, picked the ball up, hurled it over to Joey.

Joey hustled in and said, "Time blue..." Blue threw up both hands.

"Let's get two." Our bench was on their feet, cheering the infielders on.

"Move him over...." Could hear the other team cheering, too.

"Play's at two...." Joey and Keenan said simultaneously. "Jinx you're it."

The next batter due up was their number five hitter. He was two for three. Again, Coach K pulled his bullhorn to his face, "Max, your way last time...."

Bobby took to his stretch, looking right at the runner, who had a panicky lead, maybe two feet at most. Bobby picked up his right leg and rocketed a two-seam fastball right down the middle.

"Strike one!" Blue called.

Bobby again, at the stretch, threw another fastball. This time it was inside and low to the right-handed hitter. I firmly believe this kid had his nine-iron in the box, or he golfed it, deep to left field, a towering foul ball, so far left that no one saw it land. "Foul ball." Blue called out. Blue held up a fist and the peace sign—swiveled around for all to see. "One more, Bobby...one more." I heard Ian throw out. Bobby took to his stretch, peered in. Fastball was the call. Scott touched the top of his helmet. He looked over to first, no action, lifted his leg, and delivered an amazing fastball, about chest high. The batter chased it....

"Strike three...." Blue called out and went into his out motion with authority.

"That's one." Bench hollered out

Scott tossed the ball to Bobby, who then put his glove between his left elbow and side, and rubbed that ball down vigorously. Drying it off with both hands, he stepped around, picked up the rosin bag, and made a few bangs on the top and bottom of his right hand. He gathered his composure and went to his set position. Scott threw down a curve ball as pre-planned. The number six hitter was due up.

Like a starter, at a triathlon, Coach K used his bullhorn. "Max your way..."

Max waved his hand, acknowledging the call. Bobby peered over to first, Keenan at short crept over a few steps to second.... The delivery was right where Scott's mitt was placed. DING was heard.

"Two!!! Get two!!!" Bench yelled out—

The fans who were sitting, just a handful, were now on their feet like the other 99% were nearly all game. A one hopper to Keenan, he looked it in, quick exchange in the glove, and he threw sidearm over to Joey covering second. Joey took the throw, and as quickly as he stepped on second, motion pulling him to third, sidearmed the ball over to Ian. Ian, doing his best Hoover vacuum impression, sucked up that one bouncer right in the glove...

"OUT!" Blue yelled out....... "OUT!!!"

I made the last entry into the scorebook—I knew this was going into the trophy case at school—the last entry after 6 to 4 to 3, was, WE WON!!!!!!

"That's three outs!" I heard Alex say, and our bench came barreling out of the dugout. The kids were running full speed to Bobby on the mound. We had just won the Super Regionals, and we were on to STATE!!!!!!! I dropped my scorebook and joined Big R and Coach K right outside the corral of kids. It was amazing to witness, we each shook each other's hands. Big R said, "One more! Starts tomorrow! Today we celebrate!"

"Be right back." With that Big R turned and headed over to the opposing coach—the two exchanged handshakes. One minute, that's all he was gone, then came over to rejoin the team in celebration. Again, that word, respect took centerstage in Russell's life—he knew what he had to do, and he did it.

I looked over to our dugout, it was 100% vacant of players. Instead, it was jam-packed with parents, grandparents, and spectators I had never seen before. And, of course, there was Jimmy Olson snapping away.

The Talk

"Why does everyone talk about the past? All that counts is tomorrow's game."

~Roberto Clemente

After shaking hands with the opposing team, and being awarded the Super Regional Trophy, all the kids picked up their gear, which was gear scattered to all corners of the ballfield. Big R took the team outside the dugout and asked them to take a knee.

"Men, today's victory is due to all of your unselfish efforts." Big R's head was held up high, and as proud, as proud could be. He continued, "TEAM—Together Everyone Achieves More." He pointed to every single player, and then pointed at Coach K and me. With parents all gathered around now, he shared. "Thank you for this W...." He then pointed to all within an earshot—making eye contact with each and every one of them. In his closing, he rattled off one last quote that he so enjoyed sharing after a W, which coach Lou Holtz used many times— "If what you did yesterday seems big, then you haven't done anything today."

"Sweats, how can I help? What can I do?" Those were the words of a winning team—what can I do?????? Like every game, once the dust settled, everyone lent a hand to clean up— "Plastics..." was in full-force. Each player grabbed a bag, each player grabbed a bat—not a single player walked empty-handed to the bus. We were all in this together.

Right outside the dugout, parents smothered their kids—hugs, and high-fives were extended all around. This was the first time the Titans had never won the Super Regional. It was a massive experience for families and our community to take in.

"Coach, can I get a few words with you, please. I am Frank Willis, with the *Harrison Tribune*." That's his name, Frank. I reeled it in. Jimmy Olson, I was thinking had a name with the face.... I just couldn't think of it for the life of me.

"Hi, Frank. Good to see you, and thanks for coming. Please, can you interview Coach Kuster and Coach Eddie—you two take it from here...." Russell shared with us both, and expressed, "It's their turn. Both of them made today happen—let's get them on record." He walked away with a bucket of balls in one hand and holding his five-year-old's hand with the other.

K and I rattled off a few answers. Honing in on discipline, teammates, unity, selflessness, and closed it with dedication.

"Mind if I get two players?"

"Sure thing." K then with his famous bullhorn, "Klaus and Scott—front and center."

"Yes, sir." Both ran up quickly...

"Boys, this is Mr. Willis with the *Harrison Tribune*, could you share a few words?"

"Yes, of course, Coach."

All the players were walking to the cheese wagon, walking side by side with dads, moms, and grandparents, younger siblings, teachers, alumni. Previous players, too, were laughing and congratulating. Everyone was talking and just having an amazing evening. I always double checked the dugout, even though I trusted the players.

Big R always stressed, "Inspect what you expect." I never was let down. On the record this little dugout had twenty-five boys in there—eating, drinking, gnawing on sunflower seeds and bubble gum. Sweats, again catering to his teammates, delivered a five-star cleaning. We never had a shop-vac, or mop, but what these kids left behind was top quality cleanliness. We could have eaten off the floor.... Ritz Carlton management would have taken notes, and a PowerPoint would have been created for the world to see—that's how we show respect.... win or lose.... but it's so much better when we win.

The Bus Ride Home

"The strength of the team is each individual member. The strength of each member is the team."

~Phil Jackson

One by one, kids exchanged a few more handshakes, hugs and high-fives with family and friends. It never failed. It was always Little Timmy on the bus first.

"We did it Mr. Figgs! We did it!!!" I could hear him through all the open windows on the bus.

"Titans crushed it today." Mr. Figgs, our bus driver, exchanged back.

"I got a stolen base today, and I scored."

"I witnessed the whole game, Timmy. Just amazing. The team should be very proud."

It was as far back in time as we could go, with this season nearly coming to an end—one game left, however, it was on our first road trip back in mid-March that Mr. Figgs was part of the family.

The bus pulled up right outside the locker room at Pond High. Mr. Figgs got out. He had been our bus driver for years upon end. His parents owned the bus company and were responsible for all the buses throughout the school district, even handling middle school and grade school.

"Welcome back, Greg! Welcome back," I said. Then we shook hands as the team hustled onboard, one after another.

A little small talk between us both commenced, going over what he had been up to.

"Just driving. Just driving."

"Hard to believe you have been doing this for thirty years."

"Wouldn't have it any other way. My dad loved this business, Mom too, and it all carried over to me and my wife after Dad retired."

"I remember your pops driving us to the games. How is your dad doing?"

"Great—he and mom downsized to a condo, just about a mile or so from here, over on Cherry Tree Lane."

"Super! Please tell him hello for me."

"I will Coach."

Bags and bats in hand, cleats dangling off backpacks, the team flew up the stairs. Coach K made his way over to the bus, gave Greg a handshake too, then proceeded up the mini staircase. Looking over my shoulder, I could see Sweats and Big R making their way up the asphalt pathway—

each one carrying something. I thought to myself, Big R was not first, he was last. Very cool I remember thinking. Last year Coach Jones was the first one on. Not today, the head coach was last.

Big R approached the bus, and I proceeded to introduce Greg to Russell.

"Coach, this is Greg Figgs."

"Yes, of course. Good to see you again, sir. You used to drive me and my team around. But that was many years ago." Handshake of course followed. Coach continued, "Thank you oh so much for driving us, the team and for being an important part of our season. If my memory serves me right, you are a Pond High grad too."

"Yes, I am."

"Sweats you know what to do." Big R pointed to him.

"I guessed on your size Mr. Figgs. Medium to Large. Here you go sir, try it on."

As Sweats handed him the hat, Greg Figgs had the biggest smile—again, something our team was not used to, that included our bus driver.

"Man, oh man—that looks great on you," Sweats said.

"Welcome to our team Greg Figgs!! Welcome to our team." Big R shook his hand, and proceeded to yell out, "ALL ABOARD."

As we all took our seats. Players in the back, coaching staff, and Sweats at the head of the bus. Greg made his final walk around the outside of the bus, came in through the folding entrance door with his ball cap on.

"Can I have everyone's attention please." Big R stood up. He grabbed Mr. Figgs and spun him around to face the team— "This is Mr. Figgs. He went to school here at Pond High, and I did a little digging. He too played baseball for the Titans.

ROARS and CHEERS were heard instantly. Everyone was clapping.

I turned, and told Coach K, "I had no idea. All these years and he never said a peep."

"Kids, Mr. Figgs is on this team—that is why we ALL gave him a hat. It symbolizes we are all in this together." Big R clapping over and over, with pats on Greg's back–redness took over the bus driver's face, who from this day forward was known as Mr. Figgs—he now had a name to his face. Not a title, but a name.

That was a special day for the whole team. Looking back, we never interacted with Mr. Figgs. Sure, us coaches did. Little Timmy always did. But the players never knew his name. He never watched one game—he just sat in the bus and read, listened to music on his phone, or took a little nap. I never once saw him in the stands.

This was Big R's team, not Jones' team—huge difference.

Big R stressed and stressed T.E.A.M—which included our bus driver.

As I took my seat, on the right side of the bus, looking out I could still see my wife waving to us. She, too, was interacting with other wives, moms, and dads. She was all in.

On que—as it always was, Mrs. Rivers approached the bus with bags full of food, and I mean bags. Her go to meal was Jimmy John's. She loved to serve up the 30-piece party box, which also included twelve half wraps. Mrs. Rivers always picked out the J.J. Gargantuan—my favorite after a big game. Turkey, roast beef, ham and with all the greens you could ask for. Chips too—salt and vinegar, plain and BBQ—and last, but not least, enough Gatorade and water to fill a trough. She never forgot the coaches and Sweats—two Cokes, one Diet Coke and a Hi-C for Sweats. She even kicked in a few snackies for the road trip. Milk Duds, Snickers, M&M's and always had red velvet, chocolate chip and oatmeal raisin cookies. We were never short. And a touch that was immediately thrown in was a Sprite for Mr. Figgs, with a twelve-inch combo meal.

"Eat it up boys! You deserve it." I said as we ate our team meal.

Years ago kids could drive themselves to a ball game. Kentucky, nearly twenty-five years ago, passed a state law that all members of high school must ride as a team on a school bus to all events—which included all sports, no matter the size. I agree with that rule. Because front and center our whole team was celebrating as a unit, one massive unit. And we were floating on cloud nine.

Midway home, as everyone settled down, Danny stood up and gave out two words. "One more!!!!"

The bus went into an enormous cheer. Franky then stood up, and rattled off, "Celebrate today. Tomorrow we are off. Monday we are back at it. We have six days to prepare, to get ready. Let's stay focused, but for now let's Rock N Roll!!!"

The bus ride home was just amazing. Cars flew by with honks and beeps and waves out the windows. It was amazing to be a part of that day. Everyone was in harmony, Big R, Coach K, and I were having a blast. The unity took center stage, and the vision became a reality. Just one more to go, one more....

State Game

"Every champion was once a contender who refused to give up."

~Rocky Balboa

Pond High vs Willcott High. That was the match of the day. It was a beautiful Saturday in Lexington, playing on a top-notch ball field with the University of Kentucky hosting the event.

For five days, our team did nothing but small ball routines. From covering first, backing up home, hitting the cutoff man—OSCAR. To bunting, hitting off the tee, batting cages, fielding a bunt, to turning a double play. In other words, it was the same practices we always conducted, nothing changed at all—NOTHING.

Big R always stressed, "Why fix something if it ain't broke."

Routine, routine—do your job, know your job, and do it with the best of your abilities.

Seven days off between games, which was no time to let up—we had to rest a few arms. But, good, solid practice continued. We started with the same five infielders and three outfielders, and this time Colton got the start. We were the home team today. We had a better regular season record, by two games, but that was enough for us to take the field first.

The stadium was packed, and I mean packed, for a 5A State Championship. I found out later that there were 5,714 fans in attendance that day. The stadium held 6,000—nearly at full capacity.

Colton was an ace on the mound—striking out five batters in the first three innings, giving up only two hits, and the key was zero runs.

Our lineup was solid. Keenan led off and was two for two through three innings. Danny, Joey, Franky, and Scott were one for two. Max in the bottom of the third, hit a towering goner. Gave us the lead 1-0.

Colton went one more inning than usual, he was really bringing it. A first and second situation was created with no outs.

Big R called for the switch, Klaus was in. And with everyone having his back, he got us out of the jam.

We only had one stolen base—Kevin took second in the fifth inning. We were manufacturing hit after hit. Nearing the bottom of the seventh we were up 3 to 1. Yes, one run scored on us, a fastball backfired. But we faced the best, with the best. It cost us a run, no big deal. We ended up getting three quick outs that inning.

It was now the eighth inning. Our team was in stride the whole time. The dugout cheering continued, but nothing like the previous game. Every single tool was used by Big R just seven days ago. Yes, this game was for the State Championship, but the last game brought out our best. This game was good, don't get me wrong, but the previous game got us here. We should have faced the other team for the State Finals, I often reflected back.

Allen, our ace fireman, was handed the ball to enter the eighth inning.... He produced two strikeouts, and created a massive, deep flyball to Bruno in right field for the third out.

We had one last bat left. Little Timmy was pinch running for Arnold on first, who had gotten a single. Kevin was up next, and as he had worked all season on his stance. He launched a homer right over the left field fence.

5-1 us, going into the top of the ninth. Again, Allen had some vicious pop to his heater. He gave up a walk, which was fine. A few calls could have gone either way. No outs. Next batter tried to lay down a bunt. Allen, off to his side, quickly grasped the ball and threw a missile to Danny on first, for one out.

Next batter hit a nice rip down third base side. Franky looked the ball into his chest, peeked over to second, runner holding, and rifled the ball over to first for the second out.

"One more!" I heard the fans yelling out. Our dugout was on its feet...

Allen got the sign. Of course, it was a fastball. He took to his stretch, made the delivery and a vicious cut was made.

"Strike one." Blue yelled out. Which was followed up by, "Strike two." Again, a massive cut, swinging for the fences was an understatement.

Allen got the ball back from Scott, two down in the dirt was called. As scripted, a curve was on the way, a slow, breaking curve it was.

"Strike three." Blue went into his K dance.

Our bench exploded out of the dugout—a pyramid was created on the pitcher's mound...One player after another topped the next, higher, and higher it went.

I looked over, and there was Jimmy Olsen on the field— "Click! Click! Click!" You could hear his high-speed lens.

Extra!! Extra!! Read all about it.

Leadership wins STATE!!

That night after the big win, *The Harrison Tribune* went into overtime mode, actually creating a Sunday edition. *The Tribune* normally only came out once a week, on Wednesday's. This time, it came out on Sunday which took the whole community by surprise. Here is the article—I left most of it out, but you will get the point.

TITANS WIN

Leadership Champs!!!!

By Frank Willis ~Senior Writer/*Harrison Tribune*

The road to State was in the very early stages back in January. The Titans baseball team was coachless. A team that had never been to state, a team that had never been to Super Regionals was lacking leadership. Pond High had two dedicated assistant coaches, but the school was looking for more, a true leader that could lift the team, the players, the coaches and create a winning program.

Out of the few coaches that applied for the program, one man, Coach Russell was awarded the head manager job. It's not every day that a college basketball coach is picked to be the head baseball coach, but that is what transpired. High school sports is not travel ball, nor is it made up of the best athletes. You take what the school gives you. You work through the process, and you create a team with the students who come out for the program.

I had been following Big R, as the players called him, for months. I have seen coaches come and go, and of course, seen coaches who overstay their visit. Victory is what every school in the nation wants, while leadership is what every school in the nation needs. Players and students alike need authentic leadership from all outlets—classroom, ballfield, home and even a summer job. It's hard today to find that right person who can be a beacon of light and develop young men.

Big R is that manager. Let me rephrase that, he is the right coach. It was game five of the season, a home game, which the Titans lost, 5 to 3. Great game, but it was what Big R did after the game that I witnessed, that built this team into champions. Two players had turned an easy routine ground balls into errors, Big R did not scold them in the moment. It wasn't until after the game, I saw him with his fungo bat, hitting ground balls to both kids, explaining what had happened, and how to correct it. Last year, no extra one-on-one took place. This year, address it NOW....

The Titans are a very well-rounded team, from ace pitchers to outfielders and infielders. But the State Championship was created within the whole team—all players, all season, got game-time experience. It was never the same nucleus of kids from the first inning to the ninth inning. Big R used all his athletes and exercised them wisely.

It was the seventh game of the year, the Titans had two home runs, and had bunted three times all in one game. As I witnessed this match, the leadoff batter clobbered a dinger, and the designated hitter laid down a bunt. After the game, I asked Big R how they won the game, and he replied, "Everyone bunts." I asked him to elaborate, and he did. "Anyone can hit, but not everyone can bunt. We work on the little things that create movement, that generate runs, and all players are included. Therefore, the whole team can lay down a bunt when need be."

As I was leaving the field that day, I noticed lacrosse sticks being carried back to the locker room. I walked up to Coach K and said, "Lacrosse sticks, what are those for?" He replied, "We use those to teach kids how to bunt. Soft hands. Look the ball in. Catch the ball with the net, then they get a bat and apply the same technique. Repetition of a drill, over and over wins games, because then, everyone can bunt."

By the tenth game, which was the next one I was able to catch, I now could see how everyone was able to bunt. There were two doubles in this game, two singles, four stolen bases, a triple, and of course two bunts. And to top it off, there were two double plays created by the Titans defense.

State Champions were created one game at a time, one practice at a time, with every single player participating. It was truly magical to witness a coach, who was a leader, and coaches who bought into his philosophy, and the players who were winning because everyone was in it together. Week after week, momentum was building. I witnessed kids smiling, witnessed parents having fun, witnessed assistant coaches having a blast—but what I witnessed over the whole season was communication skills from the dugout to the field, from coach to player, player to coach. It truly is fascinating to bring home a trophy of this magnitude.

Pond High has a gifted manager, excellent baseball coaches, and they have the best baseball team. A team created on Big R's philosophy, that Everyone Bunts.

A philosophy that when you work together, work on the small stuff and communicate, you will generate Wins.

In this case, you will generate STATE CHAMPS!

Author Note

I have a true passion for the word leadership—I never truly understood the word as a young man playing knothole baseball in Cincinnati, Ohio. I grew up in a family of ball players. My dad was drafted out of high school by the Phillies, but didn't go due to Vietnam. He attended the University of Cincinnati, playing third base. My dad's brother, Ron, played for the Midland Redskins baseball team, in the very early years. Midland was created in 1966, by Joe Hayden—the Redskins went on to win 17 Connie Mack World Series Championships. Over time, they have generated 100+ MLB players, 2 being Hall of Fame Players.... I grew up playing nothing but baseball, I love the game with all my heart. I grew up with the Big Red Machine. All I wanted to be was a Red. I played baseball from kindergarten all the way through my senior year of high school.

My dad got hurt multiple times in college. He never made it to the big-leagues, but he did play semi-pro baseball. When we lived in Columbus, Indiana he coached a high school team. When we moved back to Cincinnati, he became assistant coach on my first little-league team, then became head coach for my brother's team for nearly eight years. There, I met coaches that influenced my life, Howie Ludwig, Gary McKee and Pat Williams. They were not my coaches, but they were a part of my life growing up—

My dad's coach at University of Cincinnati was Glenn Sample. Coach Samples' number is retired and is located on the left field wall of UC Baseball Stadium—my dad's youth knothole ambassador was a man named Winchell Smith. He oversaw the umpires on the Eastside of Cincinnati, and also was a coach for the Midland Chiefs, a team I played for. But during my junior year, pitching a no-hitter, I threw my arm out. My dad spoke so highly of them both. I never met Mr. Sample, but Winchell Smith was a big part of my life, because I umpired for three years.

Barry Martin Sr—was the dad of one of my buddies, Barry Martin Jr. He and I would go head-to-head. This guy was a beast; could hit, throw, and could cover some ground out at third. Barry played Division 1 baseball. Today he is a high school coach, and also coaches for the Midland organization. His dad was a youth coach as well. My dad and Barry Sr. were buddies. I very much looked up to Mr. Martin. He was an excellent leader.

Today I am fifty-five years old. Looking back, I had the best leaders on and off the field. From John McManus, my first baseball coach at age seven. To Ray Ayres, my high school coach, who took us to State Runner-Up in 1988. I was on a traveling baseball team, too. Going all over Ohio, Kentucky, Tennessee, Indiana, where I had a great coach named Jim Ast—whose son, Doug, is assistant coach on University of Cincinnati Clermont Basketball Team. He and I played amazing ball together.

Today I look back, not with "glory day" glasses, but with a fond respect for those who taught me so much—from running laps around a middle school building, because I was running my mouth. Thank you, Mr. Schwartz. To eating a cricket so we could wrap up football practice ten minutes early with Coach Ayers in high school.

I so wanted to be a cop, because of my assistant Knothole baseball coach, Mr. Berger. He was a Cincinnati Police Officer, a tough guy, too. I learned balance on a simple exercise in youth soccer. I practiced it so much on my own, I would kick a soccer ball up in the air, and juggle it with my feet for about five minutes, because Mr. Kirby, my assistant soccer coach, hammered that drill—I actually scored a goal, from one end of the field to the other at the age of ten, because he taught me how to control the ball. My love for the U.S. Military, came from youth baseball coach Terry Zimmerman. He was in the Coast Guard—no one in my family was in the military, and at a young age he influenced me.

No fear was taught to me by Phil Wilhoit. I was a great pitcher, then when I made his team he threw me behind home plate—he created a catcher. He took me out of my comfort zone, and I still remember the first practice, I was plowed over.

My eighth-grade baseball coach, Gary Pierson, who was also my history teacher, was one of my best buddies—but he did not play any favorites. One day in class, me and this girl, who I had a crush on, were chatting it up. Must have been around 10 a.m. He said, "Jimmy and Gina.

Go drag the baseball field—if you are going to run your mouths, I'll put you both to work." Today, that girl is my wife.

I have learned a great deal from coaches in my life. I learned that failure is not final. I learned respect for others, Yes Sir! Action supersedes motion, accountability, communication, listening, trusting one another, teamwork, team effort—Those are just a few.

The one I hold dear to my heart, is discipline through humor. Gary Pierson did this the best. His practices were a well-oiled machine, and along with his assistants who were diligent and precise on what their game plan was. If a player, including me, did something wrong, immediately it was humor for Mr. P, with a correction, and action.

It was never NO. It was, let me show you. He took practice very seriously, but to an eighth grader he kept his wits about him and connected with us with humor. He would laugh right along with us. Practice was hard, but it was fun. We all learned a ton that year, even beating our rival school team two times that season, a team Mr. Pierson lost to numerous times. We were runner-up CYO Champs–I cost us the final out, trying to steal third base.

Mr. P always told me, if he had to do it ten more times, he would have run it again. Yes, I was caught stealing third, but his philosophy was baseball always needed to be pushed past its limits—the odds would be in our favor, eventually. Coaching and leadership, as well as management and leadership all go hand-in-hand. You can't have just one, you must have both to be a thriving business or team.

The fictional story you read is based on numerous memories I have with coaches, friends, teams, the Navy, firefighters, my fraternity, ushering for the Reds and Bearcats, my family, my daughter, and my wife. The biggest asset was playing baseball, watching baseball, and being a part of baseball my whole life. I just love baseball and leadership.

Thank You

First off, I would like to thank my alma mater, McNicholas High School, and its baseball program. It has been years since I was around indoor practices, batting cages and seeing tees in action, and for over two seasons, I was given access to their practices, and got to see first-hand what a well-oiled machine looks like. Timing is everything—drill after drill, keep it simple in motion—I managed to catch eight pre-season games, and over twenty regular season games. I took notes, not only on McNick, but on the opposing teams, as well. Thank you McNick, thank you for allowing me to shadow a winning program.

Second, I would like to thank my buddy and my teammate Barry Martin Jr. He and I met all winter long, sharing and creating stories that would take this book to a polished form. His knowledge of baseball, knowledge of coaching, and leadership always creates a wining program. He once told me, that when a former player reaches out to him years later, he knew he did his job well. He knew he had a positive impact.

Third, I would like to thank Richard Kohrs for his first round of editing—Way too many quotation marks, commas, nouns, and adjectives for me to keep up with.

Fourth, I would like to thank Pat Williams. Pat is the man behind me writing books. I met Pat years ago in Cincinnati. At the time he was Sr. VP of the Orlando Magic. He gave a motivational speech, in which he said to us all, "Grab fifteen." Meaning, read for fifteen minutes a day, it will change your life. Now I am not a reader at all, I thought. Then I won a copy of his latest book at the time, *Extreme Dreams Depend on Teams*—took me one month to read it. He told me that when I finished the book to email him. I did, and he responded back with, "read another one." That year I read over one hundred books. Pat and I built a very solid relationship, one that I cherish with all my heart. Pat passed away in the summer of 2024 at the age of 84. I miss our interaction very much, but I cherish his leadership skills every day.

Fifth, I'd like to thank every single knothole, high-school, middle-school, grade-school, travel, college, semi-pro, minor-league, and big-league coach throughout the world. It takes effort, discipline, and commitment to teach values to our youth. Paid or unpaid, it doesn't matter—you are the guidepost kids are seeking. You are their example, and I truly thank you.

Sixth, I would like to thank my wife Gina—an avid reader, with a prolific knowledge and gift of seeing the bigger picture—developing innings more in depth and elevating the individuality of each character. Thank you PG, you motivate me to be more creative. I love you, best friend.

Recommended Reading

Who Coached The Coaches?
~By Andrew Herdliska

How To Be The Ultimate Teammate
~By Pat Williams

You Don't Need a Title to Be a Leader
~By Mark Sanborn

How To Lead When You're Not In Charge
~By Clay Scroggins

First Fast Fearless: How To Lead Like A Navy Seal
~By Brian "Iron Ed" Hiner

The Ultimate Coaches' Career Manual
~By Pat Williams

High Road Leadership
~By John Maxwell

The Wisdom Of The Bullfrog: Leadership Made Simple (But Not Easy)
~By Admiral William H. McRaven

The One Minute Manager Meets the Monkey
~By Ken Blanchard

Extreme Dreams Depend on Teams
~By Pat Williams

About the Author

Jim Serger graduated from the University of Cincinnati and was a Delta Tau Delta Fraternity member. Having served four years in the U.S. Navy, Jim lived in Japan for four years and served onboard the USS Independence (CV-62). He has backpacked throughout Asia numerous times, climbed Mt. Fuji, and has completed two marathons (2017 and 2020). He worked at a little convenient store for six years in high school and college, and in the packaged ice industry for eighteen years after the Navy. Jim was an operations manager serving in the aviation industry for seven years. In 2012, he rode a bicycle from Carmel, Indiana to Orlando, Florida for charity. Jim was a contributing writer to the *Current in Carmel* newspaper from 2016-2021. He was awarded the Fire Chief Commendation Award in 2023, 2024, and 2025 by the New Richmond, Ohio Fire Department. Jim also received the Citizen of the Year Award in 2024 by The Village of New Richmond, Ohio.

Jim has written nine other books: *Go the Distance* (2011), *2000 Miles on Wisdom* (2014), *Next in Line Please* (2016), *The True Facts Trivia Game: For Fans of Fox News* (2021), *A Tale of Two College Graduates Who Landed the Interview: Amy and Jeff* (2022), *9:11 A Time to Always Remember* (2022), *Jump: 40th Anniversary of Attending the "1984" Van Halen Concert* (2023), *9:11 A Time to Always Remember: Bond of Firefighters* (2024), *9:11 A Time To Always Remember: Salute to Service* (2025).

Jim's work has appeared in *Epoch Times*, *Fox News Radio*, *Fox News Digital*, *Fox & Friends Weekend*, *Newsmax*, *Success Magazine*, *ABC New York,* and numerous other outlets.

Jim currently is a Cincinnati Reds usher, as well as a University of Cincinnati Football and Basketball usher. He is the proud father of a twenty-one-year-old daughter and is married to the love of his life. Jim lives in New Richmond, Ohio.

For more information, please visit JimSerger.com

About Red Bike Publishing

Red Bike Publishing provides high quality books which can be found at www.redbikepublishing.com.

PUBLISHING

Get Rich in a Niche-The Insider's Guide to Self-Publishing in a Specialized Industry

OTHER TOPICS

1. Rainy Street Stories-Reflections on Secret Wars, Espionage and Terrorism
2. Around the Corner
3. 2000 Miles On Wisdom
4. Next in Line Please
5. Blue Jacket
6. Jump 40th Anniversary of attending the "1984" Van Halen Concert
7. 9-11 A Time To Always Remember
8. 9-11 A Time To Always Remember Bond of Firefighters
9. 9-11 A Time To Always Remember Salute To Service

NOVELS

1. Commitment-A Novel
2. Devoted

SECURITY BOOKS AND TRAINING

1. How to Get U.S. Government Contracts and Classified Work
2. Insider's Guide to Security Clearances
3. Establish an Insider Threat Program Under NISPOM

www.ingramcontent.com/pod-product-compliance
Lightning Source LLC
LaVergne TN
LVHW020043110826
845155LV00029B/615

* 9 7 8 1 9 3 6 8 0 0 5 6 8 *